Montréal

a City Steeped in History

Guide to Nationally
Significant Places,
Persons and Events
on the Island of Montréal

HERITAGE GUIDE

CONTENTS

TOURS

CONTENTS

Did you know that the first steamboat built in Canada, the *Accommodation*, is commemorated in Montréal?

Did you know that George Beers, an eminent Montréal dentist, set the rules for lacrosse and popularized the game in the 19th century?

Did you know that Saint-Laurent Boulevard, Mount Royal Cemetery and several churches, like Saint Patrick's Basilica, are national historic sites?

These are only a few examples of places, persons and events of national historic significance on the Island of Montréal that are part of Parks Canada's national historic sites system plan. You can learn more about them by reading this guide, which contains over 100 historical entries, as well as a rich and varied selection of illustrations. It also provides a summary of the history of Montréal and includes alphabetical and thematic indexes that can be used to design your own tours.

If you're interested in history, simply a bit curious, feel strongly about heritage protection or are just looking for a different way to visit Montréal, then this guide is for you!

Did you know that a plaque at Pierre Elliot Trudeau International Airport recalls the commissioning of the *Norseman*, an airplane that won renown in Canada's Far North and in Europe during the Second World War?

Did you know that Howie Morenz, a star player with the Montreal Canadiens Hockey Club in the 1920s and 1930s, is commemorated by a plaque unveiled at the Forum in 1978?

Did you know that the Government of Canada has recognized the historic importance of a number of events in the Montréal area, such as the construction of the Victoria Tubular Bridge in 1859 and the signing of the Great Peace of Montréal in 1701?

Take a look at the following pages: you'll make some amazing discoveries!

A RICH AND FASCINATING HERITAGE

5

This guide is divided into three sections suggesting tours based on the geographical proximity of sites designated for places, persons or events of national historic significance in three different parts of the Island of Montréal.

- For **OLD MONTRÉAL** and the surrounding area, it proposes three tours that can easily be done on foot;
- for DOWNTOWN, it focuses on four areas with a high concentration of designations that are within ready reach by metro: 1. the area around Windsor Station and Dorchester Square; 2. northwestern downtown; 3. the McGill University sector; and 4. eastern downtown, along with several churches, Place des Arts and the Monument-National;
- in regard to **THE ISLAND OF MONTRÉAL**, the guide discusses five zones that you can also reach by metro or by bus, perhaps while going on a picnic or other type of outing: 1. from the Botanical Garden to the city's cemeteries; 2. from the Lachine Canal to Villa Maria; 3. the Lachine Rapids; 4. the western part of the island; and 5. the city's outskirts.

Several maps show the location of the various designations made by the Historic Sites and Monuments Board of Canada, irrespective of whether they are marked by a commemorative plaque or not. In addition, inset maps are provided in the upper right-hand corner of all odd-numbered pages. For ease of understanding, many titles of the various designations have been adapted in English and may differ from those inscribed on the commemorative plaques.

Two indexes, one alphabetical and the other thematic, make it easier to find the various designations and prepare personalized tours.

Example: Old Montréal

Presentation of the area and tour maps

Presentation of the tour with inset maps and historical entries

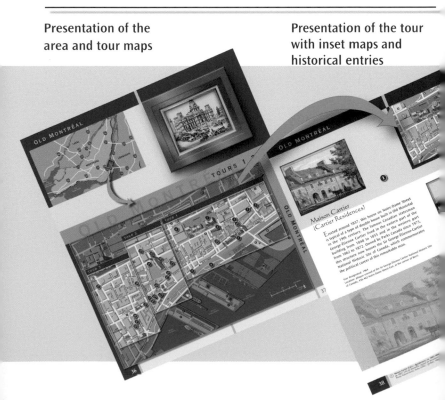

THE ISLAND OF MONTRÉAL

DOWNTOWN

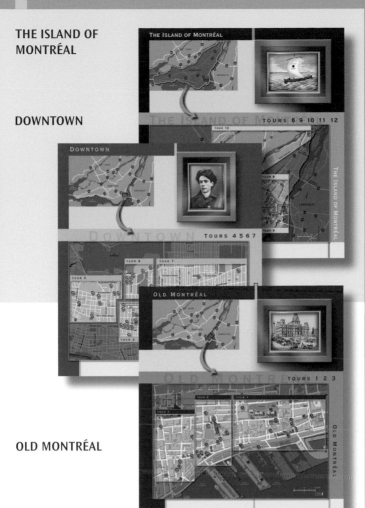

OLD MONTRÉAL

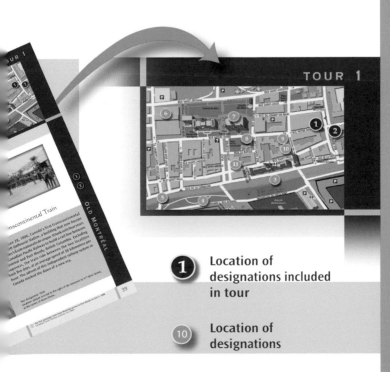

① **Location of designations included in tour**

⑩ **Location of designations**

I would first like to thank Pierre Beaudet and Michel Filteau for their ceaseless efforts to have the guide published. I would also like to thank a number of other people who participated in this project: Johanne Lachance and Normand Lafrenière, who did part of the research and wrote a number of the historical entries; all the persons who revised the text; Pierre Rochon, who drew the maps; Jean Drolet, who digitized the photographs; and Bernard Pelletier, who developed the guide's outstanding design.

As well, I would like to extend a special thank you to Doris Drolet-Dubé for preparing and maintaining the database, conducting documentary research and playing such an active role in this enterprise. I am also grateful to all the persons and institutions who contributed to the rich visual aspect of this guide. The excellent translation in English is the work of Alison McGain and Jane Macaulay.

Lastly, I would like to stress the invaluable collaboration of the Société de développement de Montréal, McCord Museum and Tourisme Montréal, all of which provided much-appreciated financial support for this project.

Rémi Chénier
Historian
Parks Canada
Quebec Service Centre

What is the National Historic Sites of Canada System Plan?

Canada's program of historical commemoration is managed by Parks Canada. The relevant minister makes designations on the recommendation of the Historic Sites and Monuments Board of Canada, created in 1919. Since the Board's inception, close to 2,000 places (145 of which are administered by Parks Canada), persons and events have been designated as being of national historic significance. Together, they form the National Historic Sites of Canada System Plan.

One of the federal government's key objectives in respect to this system is to ensure that it reflects the country's evolving history and heritage and accurately mirrors Canadians' interests and priorities in this regard. Over 80% of requests for designation are submitted by the general public; the remainder are made by Parks Canada and other federal departments.

NATIONAL HISTORIC SITES OF CANADA THEMATIC FRAMEWORK

PEOPLING THE LAND
- Canada's Earliest inhabitants
- Migration and Immigration
- Settlement
- People and the Environment

GOVERNING CANADA
- Politics and Political Processes
- Government Institutions
- Security and Law
- Military and Defence
- Canada and the World

DEVELOPING ECONOMIES
- Hunting and Gathering
- Extraction and Production
- Trade and Commerce
- Technology and Engineering
- Labour
- Communications and Transportation

BUILDING SOCIAL AND COMMUNITY LIFE
- Community Organizations
- Religious Institutions
- Education and Social Well-Being
- Social Movements

EXPRESSING INTELLECTUAL AND CULTURAL LIFE
- Learning and the Arts
- Architecture and Design
- Science
- Sports and Leisure
- Philosophy and Spirituality

DESIGNATIONS OF NATIONAL HISTORIC SIGNIFICANCE IN CANADA (1919-2003)

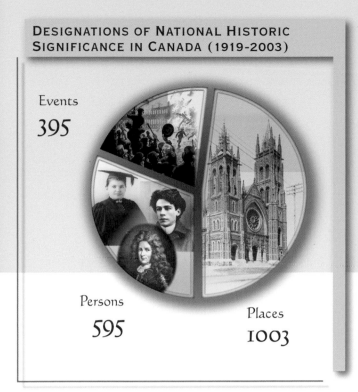

Events
395

Persons
595

Places
1003

Parks Canada's system plan, as reviewed in October 2000, proposes a global approach to understanding Canada's history, based on five themes providing a framework for the selection of designations. In response to public consultations on heritage protection and to fill certain gaps in public requests for designation, Parks Canada has set three commemorative priorities: Aboriginal history, the history of ethnocultural communities and women's history.

The system plan should reflect the country's evolving history and heritage.

NATIONAL HISTORIC SITE OF CANADA SYSTEM PLAN

HISTORIC SITES AND MONUMENTS BOARD OF CANADA

The Historic Sites and Monuments Board of Canada currently has 20 members. Both Quebec and Ontario have two representatives, while the other provinces and the three territories (Yukon, Northwest Territories and Nunavut) each have one.

Any aspect of Canada's history may be declared of national historic significance. Places, persons or events may be designated if they have had a nationally significant effect on the country's history or illustrate a nationally important aspect of it. To be eligible, places (archaeological sites, structures, buildings or groups of buildings, districts or cultural landscapes) must have been created before 1975, while persons must have been deceased for at least 25 years, except in the case of Canadian prime ministers, who are eligible for commemoration immediately after their death.

VARIOUS TYPES OF PLAQUES (1923-2003)

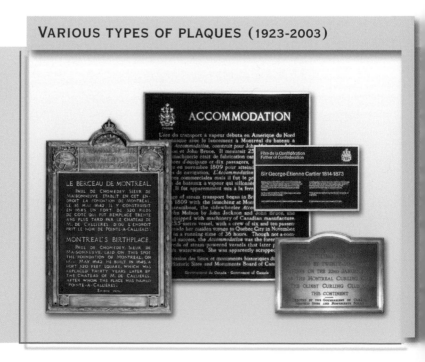

Various types of plaques (1923-2003).
Photos: Rémi Chénier, Parks Canada, Québec, 1991.

Based on the Board's recommendations, commemoration may take various forms: the erection of a plaque, the construction of a monument, or a cost-sharing agreement for the preservation or presentation of a site declared to be of national historic significance. The erection of a bilingual plaque is the most common form of commemoration.

The First Members of the Historic Sites and Monuments Board of Canada.
Cover of the Board's Minutes, November 1979, by R. Huggins of Parks Canada.

The Island of Montréal enjoys a special geographic situation that has had an impact on the history of both the island and the city of Montréal. It is located at the confluence of the St. Lawrence and Ottawa rivers and is bounded to the north by the Rivière des Prairies and to the south by the St. Lawrence River and Lake Saint-Louis. Owing to the proximity of these navigable waterways, Montréal is a gateway to the continent of North America and to one of Canada's most fertile farming regions. For many years, Montréal was its main administrative, economic, military and religious centre.

Over 20% of all the designations of national historic significance in Canada concern the province of Quebec. The Island of Montréal alone boasts 113 designations, or almost one-third of all designations in the province and 6% of those in the country as a whole. These figures clearly reflect the importance of the Island of Montréal in the history of both Quebec and Canada.

Up to the 1990s, designations on the Island of Montréal conformed to a traditional interpretation of Canadian history, particularly with

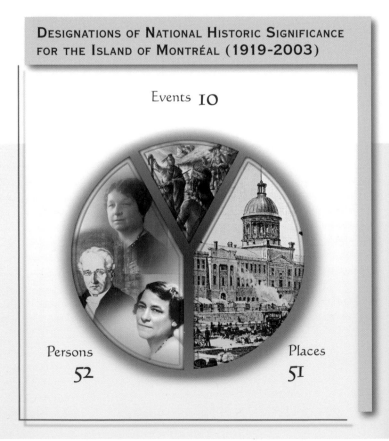

DESIGNATIONS OF NATIONAL HISTORIC SIGNIFICANCE
FOR THE ISLAND OF MONTRÉAL (1919-2003)

Events 10

Persons 52

Places 51

regard to aboriginal people, ethnocultural communities and women. This is due to the fact that public requests for designation do not always keep pace with changes and new directions in the study of history. It should also be said that the composition and commemorative priorities of the Historic Sites and Monuments Board have evolved since 1919.

Designations on the Island of Montréal can be divided fairly evenly into three main historical periods: the French Regime, the British Regime and the Province of Canada, and Modern Canada. Obviously, certain designations, such as the Saint-Laurent Boulevard Historic District, overlap two or more of these periods.

Based on the designations made for the French Regime (1534-1760), the Board seems to have focused attention for the first 20 years of its existence on exploration (*Hochelaga,*

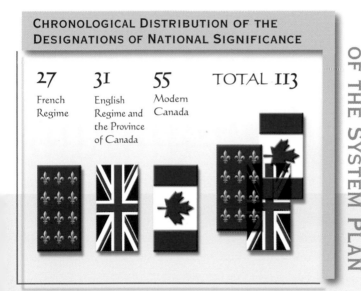

CHRONOLOGICAL DISTRIBUTION OF THE DESIGNATIONS OF NATIONAL SIGNIFICANCE

27 French Regime

31 English Regime and the Province of Canada

55 Modern Canada

TOTAL 113

Cavelier de La Salle, Voyageurs[1], etc.), colonization efforts and the first settlements (*The Origins of Montréal*), and military affairs and conflicts with aboriginal peoples (*Battle of Rivière-des-Prairies, Battle of the Lake of Two Mountains, Le Moyne d'Iberville* and *the Lachine Massacre*). Subsequently, it does not seem to have had any special focus, but simply commemorated several places (*Lachine Rapids, Sulpician Seminary Gardens, Sulpician Towers* and *Château Ramezay*)

---

1 Words in italics refer to entries in the tour section of the guide that provide brief historical summaries for each designation.

and a number of important personalities (*Marguerite Bourgeoys, Chomedey de Maisonneuve, Jeanne Mance,* etc.). It should be noted that a study on the contribution of religious communities in Canada led to the designation, in 1988, of the *Society of Jesus* (the Jesuits), the *Congrégation de Notre-Dame* and the *Grey Nuns of Montréal*. More recently, the commemoration of the *Great Peace of Montréal* in 1701 paid tribute to its principal architects: *Callière* and *Kondiaronk*.

Like the designations for the French Regime, those for the British Regime and the Province of Canada (1760-1867) are associated primarily with persons and places. They mainly concern Montréal's English-speaking community (English, Scottish and Irish), politics and business, and the religious sphere. Several designations are associated with transport, industry and technology, while others focus on sports (*Royal Montreal Curling Club, George Beers* and lacrosse) or on literature and art (*Michel Bibaud* and *William Notman*). Once again, these designations reflect a traditional view of history, while testifying to the predominant values of society at a given time.

Certain buildings have also been recognized as being of national historic significance, and they represent a wide range of architectural styles:[2] Neoclassical (*Bonsecours Market*), Gothic Revival (*Saint Patrick's Basilica, Notre-Dame Basilica, Christ Church Cathedral* and *Trafalgar Lodge*) and Palladian (*Old Custom House*). Two cemeteries, namely, *Mount Royal* and *Notre-Dame-des-Neiges*, have been commemorated as well.

More than half of the designations for Modern Canada, that is, for the period from Confederation in 1867 to today, are associated with persons, including three of the Fathers of Confederation (*George-Étienne Cartier, Thomas D'Arcy McGee* and *Alexander Tilloch Galt*). Merchants and businessmen, like those who worked for the Canadian Pacific Railway, are well represented by such names as *Macaulay, Macdonald, Rose, Smith, Stephen* and *Van Horne*. In addition, several designations are for internationally renowned leaders in the fields of medicine (*Abbott, Archibald, Osler, Penfield* and *Selye*) and science (*Adams, Brother Marie-Victorin, Kennedy* and *Rutherford*); most of these people worked at McGill University. Lastly, a number of designations of national historic significance concern personalities from various sectors associated with the world of art and literature, including journalism (*Bourassa*), music (*Champagne* and *Pelletier*), museology (*McCord*), painting (*Morrice*) and poetry (*Nelligan*).

---

2 See the summary of architectural styles below.

Certain designations associated with Modern Canada reflect Parks Canada's commemorative priorities. For example, the plaque on *Railway Porters and their Unions* recalls the struggle waged by Black people for union representation and the protection of human rights. The names *Maude Abbott, Marie Lacoste-Gérin-Lajoie, Margaret Ridley Charlton* and *Idola Saint-Jean* are all associated with women who dedicated themselves to women's emancipation. The *Hersey* and *Mailloux* pavilions pay tribute to the nursing profession.

Some 20 designations highlight various architectural styles: Arts and Crafts (*Senneville Historic District*), Art Deco (*Outremont Theatre*), Beaux-Arts (*Montreal Masonic Memorial Temple, Rialto Theatre*), Eclecticism (*Monument-National*), Baroque Revival (*Marie-Reine-du-Monde Basilica-Cathedral*), Gothic Revival (*Wilson Chambers, St. George's Anglican Church, St. James United Church*), Queen Anne Revival (*Marlborough Apartments, Bank of Montreal Building, H. Vincent Meredith Residence*), Romanesque Revival (*Windsor Station, Erskine and American United Church, Church of Notre-Dame-de-la-Défense*), Renaissance Revival (*George Stephen House*) and Second Empire (*Montréal City Hall, Van Horne-Shaughnessy House*). The various buildings associated with these styles were often the work of certain architects and decorators active in Montréal, such as Bourgeau, Briffa, Mesnard, Nincheri, Perrault, Thomas, and Maxwell.

Bonsecours Market, Montréal, ca. 1920, Herbert Raine.
NAC, e000943146 (Peter Winkworth Collection of Canadiana).

MONTRÉAL, AT THE HEART OF THE SYSTEM PLAN

The designations of national historic significance on the Island of Montréal cover the three main periods in the history of Montréal.

The French Regime

The plaque commemorating *Hochelaga* recalls the fact that Jacques Cartier, "the discoverer of Canada," visited the Island of Montréal and the Iroquoian village of Hochelaga during his second voyage to this part of the world in 1535. He probably returned to the region in 1541 to draw a map of the *Lachine Rapids*. In 1603 Samuel de Champlain, who later founded Québec City, explored the St. Lawrence River above the rapids. Eight years later, he cleared a plot of land in a place he named Place Royale and which is now known as Pointe-à-Callière.

The Origins of Montréal plaque recounts the founding of Ville-Marie by *Paul de Chomedey de Maisonneuve, Jeanne Mance* and a group of settlers on May 17, 1642, under the aegis of the Société de Notre-Dame de Montréal for the purpose of converting the "savages." This missionary colony was the most westerly settlement in New France.

The Iroquois[3] attacked the settlement for the first time in 1643, the year Louis d'Ailleboust de Coulonge built a fort at Pointe-à-Callière. The situation became so difficult for the colonists that by 1650 they no longer dared leave the fort. The arrival of new settlers in 1653 and 1659 ensured the settlement's survival.

---

3 A powerful confederation of five Aboriginal nations who originally inhabited the northern part of the state of New York. They initially allied themselves with the Dutch and then with the British, as they battled the French for control of the fur trade and to maintain their role of intermediaries with other Aboriginal nations.

The fur trade acquired considerable importance very early in the history of Ville-Marie, with the settlement forming the hub of a trade network involving Amerindians who descended the Ottawa and St. Lawrence rivers every year to exchange furs. In fact, the fur trade soon played a vital role in the local economy, especially since the Société de Notre-Dame was in financial trouble and was having difficulty covering the settlement's expenses. On March 9, 1663, it was obliged to cede the seigneury of the Island of Montréal to the Sulpician Seminary.

This early period was also marked by the arrival of various religious communities. The Jesuit missionaries (*Society of Jesus*) were followed by the Sulpicians in 1657 (*Sulpician Seminary Gardens, Sulpician Towers*). *Marguerite Bourgeoys* arrived in 1653 and founded the *Congrégation de Notre-Dame* in 1658; the following year, the Religious Hospitallers of St. Joseph made their way to the settlement.

From the outset, the religious communities occupied vast properties, which, until the late 19th century, played a role in shaping the landscape of Montréal. The communities also owned a number of large buildings. The settlement's parish church was inaugurated in 1683 and construction began on the new Sulpician Seminary in 1684. The hospital known as the Hôtel-Dieu, erected by *Jeanne Mance*, was replaced by a stone structure between 1689 and 1694; however, the new building was destroyed by fire in 1695, and the hospital was immediately rebuilt. The *Congrégation de Notre-Dame*, founded in 1658, moved to new quarters in 1684. In 1692 the Recollets settled in the western part of the city, while the Jesuits (*Society of Jesus*), who had returned to the colony that same year, settled in the eastern part, outside the palisade. *Mother Marie-Marguerite d'Youville* founded the *Grey Nuns of Montréal* in 1737.

In 1666 the new seigneurs of the Island of Montréal, the Sulpicians, began to divide up their property to allow colonists to settle and farm it. The first rural parish, Pointe-aux-Trembles, was created in the eastern part of the island in 1674, while the parish of Lachine was founded in the western part in 1676. The latter parish was destroyed, however, in 1689 (*Lachine Massacre*). In 1687 another parish by the name of Rivière-des-Prairies was founded in the northeast (*Battle of Rivière-des-Prairies*). The northern part of the island developed more rapidly than the southwestern part, and towards the end of the 17th century, the Sulpicians began to grant lots in the interior.

After 1670 the name Montréal gradually began to replace that of Ville-Marie, although the latter remained in use until as late as 1685. The Sulpicians' Father Superior, François Dollier de Casson, drew up the first street plan for the city in 1672, and most of the streets laid out at that time still exist today. There were 152 houses in Montréal in 1697, and there were 400 in 1731, despite the huge fire that had destroyed 160 homes and the Hôtel-Dieu 10 years earlier.

Montréal was a nerve centre during the French Regime. It served as a military base for stationing troops, launching expeditions against the British colonies and their Five Nations allies (the Iroquois) and establishing forts in New France's interior, particularly around the Great Lakes. It also played a leading role in controlling the fur trade and in the conduct of diplomatic relations, particularly with aboriginal peoples, as shown by the negotiations that led to the *Great Peace of Montréal* in 1701 (*Callière* and *Kondiaronk*).

The city's military role was bolstered by the construction of fortifications that replaced the redoubts and small forts built in the early days of the settlement. The new fortifications were designed to protect the city from two enemies: the Iroquois, who resumed their raids with renewed vigour after the truce of 1667-1680 (*Lachine Massacre, Battle of the Lake of Two Mountains, Battle of Rivière-des-Prairies*), and troops from the British colonies. A palisade was erected in 1687-1689, and then in 1693 Governor *Callière* decided to fortify the mill on Saint-Louis Hill, to the east of the palisade. The wooden enceinte was enlarged in 1699 and 1709 to incorporate the

The city's military role was bolstered by the construction of fortifications that replaced the redoubts and small forts built in the early days of the settlement.

"citadel" and part of the Bonsecours suburb. It was replaced by a stone wall between 1717 and 1744.

The population grew only slightly in *Maisonneuve*'s day. However, by 1663 the city had 596 inhabitants, and in 1665 the number rose with the arrival of soldiers from the Carignan-Salières Regiment, sent to the colony to eliminate the Iroquois threat. A total of 1,200 people lived in the city in 1700 and 4,000 in 1754. Over 100 houses were ravaged by fire in 1721, after which all new homes were built in stone. The city thus acquired a new appearance, which persisted after the British Conquest of 1760.

Montréal from the Mountain, Oct. 15, 1784, James Peachey (detail).
NAC, e000835923 (Peter Winkworth Collection of Canadiana).

The British Regime and the Province of Canada

The Conquest led to a change-over in the city's elite and the creation of a business and financial network that benefited the new English-speaking entrepreneurs. In the late 18th century, the bourgeoisie was dominated by fur merchants. The North West Company, founded in 1779, had a monopoly over commercial activities in Montréal by 1804, and in 1821 it merged with the Hudson's Bay Company (*Lachine Stone Warehouse*). After 1780, even though the fur trade remained the main economic activity, the wheat, timber and potash trades began to expand, and this trend continued until the 1860s.

In 1765 and 1768 the city was again destroyed by two major fires, and then in 1775-1776, it was invaded by the Americans. With the arrival of Loyalists after 1783 and the growth of the suburbs, the population continued to increase; by 1800 there were 9,000 inhabitants. The city of Montréal was created in 1792; it comprised not only the area within the fortifications, but also the suburbs and a large part of the surrounding countryside, except Mount Royal.

From 1800 to 1850 Montréal was the most important city in British North America. However, in Montréal as in the rest of the colony, this period was a time of trouble and upheaval. Although the War of 1812 with the United States had stimulated the city's economy, the Montréal area was particularly hard hit by the Rebellion of 1837-1838 (*Louis-Joseph Papineau, Maison Papineau*). In 1840, the Province of Canada was created by the union of Upper and Lower Canada (*Augustin Cuvillier, Sir Louis-Hippolyte LaFontaine*). In

1849 the buildings that housed the *Parliament of the Province of Canada*, which was holding its sessions in Montréal at the time, were set on fire during a riot (*James Bruce, Lord Elgin*).

After the Conquest and until 1833, and then from 1836 to 1840, Montréal was administered by justices of the peace. Jacques Viger was elected mayor in 1833, the year the city's motto, *Concordia Salus* (salvation through harmony), was adopted; Viger would remain in office until 1836. A system of municipal government based on the principle of incorporation was introduced in 1840. Under the Act of 1845 the city was divided into nine wards, which remained in existence until 1899: the old city was divided into three wards (East, Centre and West) and the surrounding area into six (Sainte-Marie, Saint-Jacques, Saint-Louis, Saint-Laurent, Saint-Antoine and Sainte-Anne). The *Bonsecours Market* served as the city hall between 1852 and 1878.

Pursuant to legislation adopted in 1801 and in response to pressure by commercial and business interests, Montréal's fortifications were demolished to ensure the city's salubrity, commodiousness and embellishment. The demolition work, which lasted until 1817, made it possible to lay out new streets, such as McGill and Des Commissaires, as well as public places, such as the hay market. It also allowed the Champ-de-Mars to be enlarged. With the levelling of Citadel Hill in 1819, Notre-Dame Street was extended and Dalhousie Square laid out. The departure of the British garrison in 1871 accelerated the decline of the city's military role.

A religious revival was initiated in the 1840s, mainly under the impetus of the Bishop of Montréal, Mgr. Ignace Bourget.[4] The movement was marked by the arrival or founding of several religious communities and institutions, namely, the *Sisters of Providence*, the *Sisters of Saint Anne* and the *Villa Maria Convent*.

4 Mgr. Bourget also initiated the construction of the *Marie-Reine-du-Monde Cathedral*, which lasted from 1870 to 1894.

The *Lachine Canal*, "the birthplace of Canadian industry," was opened to navigation in 1824, even though its construction was not completed until the following year. It was enlarged in the 1840s, when the St. Lawrence canal system was extended to the Great Lakes. The next few decades witnessed the establishment of industrial facilities along the *Lachine Canal* and the expansion of the railway system (founding of the Grand Trunk Railway in 1852). This industrial and railway boom, coupled with the spinoffs from the canal's construction, transformed the Sainte-Anne Ward.

The transportation sector underwent remarkable development in the first half of the 19th century, and Montréal strove to play a leading role in trade between North America, Great Britain and Europe. It became Canada's transportation hub, due not only to the *Lachine Rapids*, which marked the boundary between marine and river navigation, but also to the integrated system of roads, canals, railroads and steamships (the *Accommodation*) put in place by Montréal merchants.

As of the 1840-1850 period, bourgeois, working-class and industrial districts grew up around the old city, which was now the centre of business and port activities. Nevertheless, it continued to serve as a centre for administrative (*Old Custom House, Bonsecours Market*), political (*Parliament of the Province of Canada*) and religious (*Grey Nuns' Hospital, Notre-Dame Basilica*) affairs.

Montréal in 1851, Augustus Kollner.
NAC, C-13448.

Industrial zones were laid out in the city's east end, between the *Molson* family's facilities and the Hochelaga neighbourhood; to the west, numerous enterprises (sawmills, flour mills and metal-working plants) set up operations around the locks of the *Lachine Canal* to take advantage of its hydraulic power (*Lachine Canal Manufacturing Complex*). The railway shops in Pointe-Saint-Charles were a source of pride to Montrealers, as was the *Victoria Bridge*, inaugurated in 1859 by the Grand Trunk Railway Company, which also manufactured railway cars and locomotives in its own Montréal workshops.

Around 1850 the Island of Montréal supplied most of the farm produce in Lower Canada, and its nine rural parishes found outlets at the city's market. However, Montréal was becoming increasingly focused on manufacturing, be it in the food, footwear, clothing or textile sectors. In addition, the city began to welcome heavy industry, based mainly on the production of transportation equipment (*Lachine Canal Manufacturing Complex*). This industrial development benefited the business and financial community, which was dominated by the banks along Saint-Jacques and Notre-Dame streets (*Augustin Cuvillier, William Molson*).

With the arrival of massive numbers of immigrants from the British colonies, particularly Ireland, between 1815 and 1850, Montréal's population grew (*Saint Patrick's Basilica*). In 1832, a cholera epidemic claimed 2,000 victims within the space of a month, and in 1847 a typhus epidemic struck. Between 1831 and 1867 the city's population became primarily English-speaking. As of the 19th century, Montréal's territory was divided along linguistic lines, with Francophones living in the east and Anglophones in the west. In 1806 two-thirds of the population lived in the suburbs and the remainder in the old city. By 1850 a mere 12% inhabited the old core, reflecting the exodus of the bourgeoisie to the suburbs. Their departure led to the creation of the "Golden Square Mile"[5] in the northwestern part of the Saint-Antoine Ward in 1840.

5 This area of roughly one square mile between Sherbrooke Street, Mount Royal Park, Côte-des-Neiges and Bleury developed especially with the arrival of railway and industrial magnates after 1860.

In 1852 when a major fire in the area of Saint-Laurent Boulevard razed 1,200 houses and left 10,000 people homeless, Montréal had 58,000 inhabitants.

Like the bourgeoisie, Montréal's churches and religious communities began to move to other parts of the city (*Villa Maria Convent, Sisters of Saint Anne*). *Christ Church Cathedral*, which had burned down in 1856, was rebuilt in the Saint-Antoine Ward, while in 1860 the Hôtel-Dieu moved to the Saint-Laurent Ward. Around 1870 the *Grey Nuns* erected a convent and a hospital between Guy Street and Dorchester Boulevard.

Modern Canada

In the late 19th century Montréal society was dominated by English and Scottish merchants and members of the bourgeoisie, including such financial, industrial and railway magnates as *George Stephen* and *William Van Horne*. It was during this period that the Canadian Pacific Railway, founded in 1881, set up its head office in Montréal's *Windsor Station*.

The influence of Montréal's elite was felt not only in the financial world but also in the city's architecture. Indeed, their tastes are reflected in the public buildings and stately homes of the period, which were inspired by the architectural styles and forms in fashion at the time in Great Britain. *George-Étienne Cartier*, a lawyer and "big businessman," was the embodiment of the French-Canadian bourgeoisie.

The many churches erected as of the mid to late 19th century testify to the wide range of religious denominations in the city (Anglican, Catholic, Jewish, Methodist, Orthodox and Presbyterian) and to the population's increasingly cosmopolitan character, even though Montréal became primarily French-speaking again after 1867, following an influx of people from the countryside. Recognized henceforth as Canada's main urban centre, the city had 107,000 inhabitants in 1871. The number of residents of British origin (Anglophones) rose between 1875 and 1900, but many Irish, mainly labourers, emigrated to the United States and Ontario. The late 19th century witnessed the arrival of Jews from Eastern Europe and Italians (*Saint-Laurent Boulevard Historic District*). Suburbs began to sprout up and some were soon annexed by the city. In 1885 an epidemic of smallpox, one of the last great scourges of the period, claimed 3,000 lives.

To keep pace with changes in navigation, business-men from Montréal's bourgeoisie devoted their energies to developing the city's port and upgrading its facilities. Indeed, sailing vessels were increasingly being replaced by steamboats. Numerous improve-ments were made to the port between 1867 and 1896: its wharfs were enlarged, docks were dug, wharf-to-rail access was made available in 1871 and grain elevators were erected by the Canadian Pacific Railway in 1885. However, as problems persisted, the Harbour Commissioners submitted a plan for renovating the port in 1877. The project was not accepted until 1891 and was implemented only in 1896. Even before 1887 "Montréal had replaced Québec City as the terminus for both deep-sea and river shipping" (*John Kennedy*).

Montréal Harbour from Custom House, ca. 1874, Alexander Henderson.
Parks Canada Collection, Quebec Service Centre.

A BRIEF HISTORY OF MONTRÉAL

As noted by historian Jean-Claude-Robert, "Montréal's economy was at its height between 1900 and 1950. . . The city accounted for over half of Quebec's manufacturing output and around 17% of that of Canada as a whole." Montréal was the country's main industrial centre, as shown by the *Lachine Canal* and its flour mills, the Redpath Sugar Refinery, the city's textile mills (*Merchants Manufacturing Company*), its metal-working sector and its willingness to embrace the latest technology. Montréal was the country's leading financial centre, as well as the hub of deep-sea shipping and rail transportation.

The process of annexing suburbs to the city initiated in the late 19th century continued into the next century. According to a 1918 report, 31 mergers had been carried out since 1883. Nonetheless, the suburbs continued to expand in several sectors, namely, Outremont (*Mount Royal Cemetery, Rialto Theatre, Outremont Theatre*), Westmount (*Church of Saint-Léon de Westmount*), Hampstead and the Town of Mount Royal.

The urban landscape changed as skyscrapers were built. In 1923 there were already some 20 buildings of this type between Place d'Armes and Saint-Pierre Street. At the

Downtown Montréal as seen from Île Sainte-Hélène in 1996.
Photo: Denis Labine. Ville de Montréal. Gestion de documents et archives. (VM94-1996-0255-070).

time, the downtown core stretched from the port to Sherbrooke Street, between Berri and Guy. The heart of the city was still Place d'Armes, which was home to *City Hall*, the Courthouse, the Stock Exchange, the main institutions, numerous office buildings and the head offices of the major banks. However, when space began to lack, many businesses moved northwest to Sainte-Catherine Street, where a second business district developed. Some even set up their head offices in the area: Sun Life, for example, built its headquarters in Dominion Square in 1918, under the presidency of *Thomas Bassett Macaulay*.

In general, the various designations on the Island of Montréal date from the period prior to World War II. However, the commemoration of the *Saint-Laurent Boulevard Historic District*, where many ethnic groups mingled and intermarried, provides a better understanding of Montréal today. Between 1950 and 1960 most immigrants came from southern Europe, while between 1970 and 1980 the majority came from the Caribbean and the Far East. In 1991, Italians, Jews and Blacks formed the three largest communities in the city, apart from those of French or British descent; Greeks, Chinese and Portuguese were the next three largest. According to the 1991 census, 45% of Quebec's population lived in the Montréal area, in keeping with a phenomenon observed since 1976.

A BRIEF HISTORY OF MONTRÉAL

Saint-Laurent Boulevard, at the corner of Sainte-Catherine Street, ca. 1910, Neurdein.
McCord Museum of Canadian History, Montréal, MP-0000.816.1.

The designations of national historic significance on the Island of Montréal testify to the diversity and richness of the national historic sites system plan. It is true, however, that the list of designations is not complete; hence the importance of calling for suggestions from the general public, who are the main source of designation applications. We hope this heritage guide will help people to formulate such applications to the Historic Sites and Monuments Board and will thereby enhance the system and foster a better understanding of our history and heritage.[6]

Montréal is still a key city in Canada, as well as a regional, cultural and financial centre. Not so long ago, it organized several events of international scope, including the 1967 World's Fair and the 1976 Olympics. The city is now undergoing major changes in the wake of the recent mergers of the island's municipalities. We therefore invite you, through the foregoing historical overview and the following sections of this guide to discover— or rediscover —

Montréal, a City Steeped in History.

Rémi Chénier

6 For further information or to suggest a topic for commemoration, please contact the Executive Secretary, Historic Sites and Monuments Board of Canada, Gatineau, Quebec, K1A 0M5, or visit the following Web site: http://www.parkscanada.pc.gc.c

Downtown Montréal as seen from Mount Royal in 1993.
Photo: Denis Labine. Ville de Montréal. Gestion de documents et archives. (VM94-1993-330-063).

Abbreviations and Further Reading

AN, AC - France, Archives nationales, Archives des colonies

ANQQ - Archives nationales du Québec à Québec

BNQ - Bibliothèque nationale du Québec

NAC - National Archives of Canada

Several books have been written on the history of Montréal. One by Raoul Blanchard, *L'ouest du Canada français, Montréal et sa région* (Montréal, Beauchemin, 1953), is somewhat dated, but still a very interesting read. A more accessible work, however, is Robert Rumilly's *Histoire de Montréal* (Montréal, Fides, 1970). There is also the authoritative work published a few years ago by Jean-Claude Robert, *Atlas historique de Montréal* (Montréal, Art global/Libre Expression, 1994). Jean-Claude Robert also worked with Paul-André Linteau on *Pre-industrial Montreal (1760 - ca. 1850)* published by the National Film Board of Canada and the National Museum of Man in 1979, with a portfolio of 30 slides.

For biographical information, readers may consult the *Dictionary of Canadian Biography* (Toronto, University of Toronto Press Ltd, 1966-), which comprises 14 volumes to date. For information on the city's architecture, they may refer to Jean-Claude Marsan's *Montreal in Evolution: Historical Analysis of the Development of Montreal's Architecture and Urban Environment* (Montréal, McGill-Queen's University Press, 1990), as well as to the series by Guy Pinard, *Montréal: son histoire, son architecture, Volumes 1 to 6* (Montréal, *La Presse* et Éditions du Méridien, 1986-) and the *Répertoire d'architecture traditionnelle sur le territoire de la Communauté urbaine de Montréal*, published in separate volumes since 1981.

Lastly, readers may also consult a number of Web sites, particularly the excellent Old Montréal site (http://www.vieux.montreal.qc.ca).

(http://www.vieux.montreal.qc.ca)

AN EVOLVING SYSTEM

This summary is based on the guide *Stylistic Terminology for Plaque Texts* prepared by the Architectural History Branch, National Historic Sites, Parks Service, Environment Canada, in 1991. It also draws on *The Buildings of Canada: A Guide to Pre-20th-Century Styles in Houses, Churches and Other Structures* by Barbara A. Humphreys and Meredith Sykes, of Parks Canada, published by Reader's Digest Association in 1980.

It is hard to assign a precise lifespan to certain architectural styles owing to the often divergent opinions of the many specialists in the field. Similarly, it is difficult to assign a specific name to certain styles or their variants because of the many terms commonly applied to them: for example, Italianate, Italian Revival, Tuscan Villa and Venetian Revival are all used to designate what is more commonly known as the Renaissance Revival style. Readers will find architectural glossaries and vocabularies in several works, including Guy Pinard's *Montréal : son histoire, son architecture*.

Art Deco
(ca. 1920-1940)

Although this style was created in France, its most enduring examples are found in North America, where they are mainly the work of French-Canadian architects. The Art Deco style is characterized by geometric, streamlined forms and the use of bare surfaces, simple decoration and classical, Egyptian and MesoAmerican motifs. It also employs bas-reliefs based on symbolic or nationalistic themes, as well as pale-toned materials.

Example: Outremont Theatre.

Arts and Crafts
(second half of the 19th century)

This movement, which first appeared in England, was derived from the Gothic Revival style and inspired by certain writings of John Ruskin that were published around 1850. Its followers advocated a return to pure architectural forms and attached considerable importance to regional traditions, artisanal techniques and local materials to ensure that buildings would be in harmony with their environment. These principles were adopted by Canada's most prominent late-19th-century architects, including brothers Edward and William Maxwell, George T. Hyde and Percy Erskine Nobbs.

Example: houses in the Senneville Historic District.

Baroque Revival
(ca. 1870-1930)

This style, which is based on French Baroque architecture in New France in the 17th and 18th centuries, is characterized by abundant ornamentation with motifs often derived from nature. Its main features are columns, pilasters, domes, pediments and steeply pitched roofs with round-headed dormers. Large buildings have a central courtyard.

Example: Marie-Reine-du-Monde Basilica-Cathedral.

Beaux-Arts
(almost the entire 20th century)

This style, which first emerged in France, gave rise to grandiose compositions. Its main characteristics are symmetrical façades, functional spatial organization and classical decorative features, particularly columns, designed to give buildings a monumental appearance. The Baroque variant of the Beaux-Arts style originated in England and makes use of such features as round-headed and broken pediments and dressed stone, carved to produce a multiplicity of sculptural effects.

Example: Montreal Masonic Memorial Temple.

Byzantine
(late 19th and early 20th centuries)

This style applies particularly to churches that display certain features of Byzantine architecture, especially domes and cupolas.

Example: St. George's Antiochian Orthodox Church.

Eclecticism
(1880-1900)

Eclecticism combines styles from different periods and countries in the façade of buildings to produce a striking visual effect. It is also characterized by the proliferation of novel, complex and imaginative forms, irregular plans and the use of several different colours on individual structures.

Example: Monument-National.

ARCHITECTURAL STYLES

Gothic Revival
(1820-early 20th century)

The pointed arch is the most characteristic feature of this style, which corresponds to an updated version of medieval architecture. Other features include buttresses, steeply pitched roofs, pinnacles, crenellation, decoratively shaped chimney stacks and shaped gables. This style has several variants that may be distinguished from one another by the types of medieval features used, the way in which features from different countries or historical periods are combined and the types of construction materials used.

Example: Christ Church Cathedral.

Neoclassical
(ca. 1820-1860)

Inspired by trends in England and France, Neoclassicism borrowed architectural forms from Greek and Roman antiquity. Some of its most distinctive features are symmetrical compositions, simple ornamentation, channelled masonry, blind arcades and flattened rusticated storeys. There is also a Greek Revival variant of the Neoclassical style, which is characterized by the use of purely Greek motifs, such as baseless Doric columns or the prostyle Greek temple form with a row of columns in front.

Example: Bonsecours Market.

Palladian
(1750s-ca. 1830)

This style was based on 18th-century British classical architecture, which in turn was influenced by the treatises of Andrea Palladio, an Italian architect of the Renaissance. Palladian buildings are symmetrical in plan and elevation, and feature projecting frontispieces, lateral wings, triangular pediments, Venetian windows (made up of three sections, of which the central one is arched) and doors framed by pilasters and surmounted by semicircular transoms or small pediments. The Palladian style borrowed numerous decorative motifs from Greek and Roman antiquity, particularly the acanthus leaf motif, baseless Doric columns, antique Ionic columns and prominent entablatures.

Example: Old Custom House.

Queen Anne Revival
(ca. 1870-1880 to the First World War)

The influence of the Queen Anne Revival style is evident especially in the architecture of private homes and to a lesser extent in that of recreational and resort buildings. It is characterized by asymmetrical plans and the manner in which shapes, materials and colours are used to create a picturesque effect. It also features a multitude of decorative details derived from classical and medieval traditions (carved pediments, decoratively shaped chimney stacks, pointed gables, moulded cornices) as well as numerous projecting and recessed elements (wings, bays, verandahs, balconies, porches).

Example: H. Vincent Meredith Residence.

Renaissance Revival
(1840-1870)

Buildings in the Renaissance Revival style are characterized mainly by their highly articulated façades, which are embellished with carved motifs creating a play of light and shadow, and are surmounted by large cornices with finely worked brackets. Windows are often arched or topped by small round-headed or triangular pediments. Buildings have three storeys — a basement, a ground floor and an attic storey — clearly marked by stringcourses.

Example: George Stephen House.

Romanesque Revival
(mid 19th century; 1880-1890)

In its early phase, the Romanesque Revival style was characterized by a return to features associated with 12th-century Norman and Lombardy architecture. By the end of the 19th century it was influenced primarily by the work of American architect H. H. Richardson. This later phase featured squat columns, corbel tables under the eaves, polychromatic and heavily textured surfaces and capitals carved with geometrical, floral or sinuous designs.

Example: Erskine and American United Church.

Second Empire
(1870s-1880s)

The most distinctive characteristic of this style of French origin is the mansard roof. Other typical features include dormer windows, round-headed windows, and large cornices with prominent brackets. Large buildings are symmetrical in composition and have projections known as pavilions.

Example: Montréal City Hall.

Vernacular

Vernacular architecture is a regional adaptation of purer styles through the use of local construction techniques and materials. In Quebec, typical features of such architecture are hipped roofs and casement windows, a legacy of the French colonial period, as well as outside metal staircases, a hallmark of houses erected in Montréal in the 19th and 20th centuries.

ARCHITECTURAL STYLES

OLD MONTRÉAL

TOURS 1 2 3

OLD MONTRÉAL

Maison Cartier (Cartier Residences)

Erected around 1837, this house on Notre-Dame Street is typical of a type of double house built in Old Montréal in the 19th century. The famous Canadian statesman George-Étienne Cartier lived in the eastern part of the building from 1848 to 1855 and in the western part from 1862 to 1872. Owned by Parks Canada since 1973, this structure now houses the Sir George-Étienne-Cartier National Historic Site of Canada, which commemorates the political career of this remarkable man.

Year designated: 1964
Location: plaque erected at the Sir George-Étienne Cartier National Historic Site of Canada, 456-462 Notre-Dame Street East, at the corner of Berri.

① Maison Cartier (Cartier Residences), ca. 1885-1890, as painted by Georges Delfosse ca. 1937. Ville de Montréal. Gestion de documents et archives. A-656-122. Photo: Robert Piette, Parks Canada, Québec, 1984.

First Transcontinental Train

On June 28, 1886, Canada's first transcontinental train left Dalhousie Station, a building that now houses Quebec's École nationale de cirque. It took only four years for the Canadian Pacific Railway to build a rail line between Montréal and Port Moody, British Columbia. Excluding stopovers, the train ride between the two localities took five days, at an average speed of 38 kilometres per hour. The advent of this independent railway system in Canada marked the dawn of a new era.

Year designated: 1939
Location: plaque erected to the right of the entrance to 417 Berri Street, at the corner of Notre-Dame.

② The first passenger train from Montréal arrives in Port Moody on July 4, 1886.
Canadian Pacific Railway Archives, NS.19991.

Bonsecours Market

A symbol of Montréal's development and prosperity, particularly in the 19th century, Bonsecours Market was for many years the structure that dominated the view seen by travellers arriving in the city's port. This Neoclassical building is primarily the work of architect William Footner, although he was relieved of his duties at one point and replaced by George Browne. The construction of this remarkable building, whose most distinctive feature is its dome, lasted from 1844 to 1860. Canada's Parliament sat here in 1849, as did Montréal's city council until 1878. At other points in its history, the public market housed a 3,000-seat concert hall, a military school and the quarters of Les Fusiliers Mont-Royal.

Year designated: 1984
Location: 350 Saint-Paul Street East;
plaque to be erected.

③ Bonsecours Market, ca. 1880.
Parks Canada Collection, Quebec Service Centre.

Sir John Kennedy (1838-1921)

John Kennedy, who came from Spencerville, in Grenville County (Upper Canada), began his career in 1863 as an apprentice with T. C. Keefer. He later worked as an assistant surveyor for the City of Montréal and, from 1875 to 1907, as chief engineer for the Montreal Harbour Commission. In the latter capacity, he played an instrumental role in the city's development by refitting the port of Montréal and dredging the St. Lawrence River between Montréal and Québec City, two major projects for which he gained considerable renown. In 1892 he became president of the Canadian Society for Civil Engineering, of which he was a founding member. His contribution to the field of engineering and his excellent work earned him many honours in both Canada and Great Britain. By the time of his death in 1921, he had acquired an excellent reputation among the members of his profession.

Year designated: 2000
Proposed location: Old Port of Montréal, in the park between De la Commune Street and the Promenade des Artistes; plaque to be erected.

OLD MONTRÉAL

④ John Kennedy, ca. 1892.
Transactions of the Canadian Society for Civil Engineering, vol. 6 (1892).

5a

Saint-Laurent Boulevard Historic District ("The Main")

Saint-Laurent Boulevard, commonly known as "the Main," is a captivating street. As of 1825 it was the most important north-south business artery on the Island of Montréal. Attracted by the street's prosperity, successive groups of immigrants from around the world took up residence here in the hope of carving out a place for themselves in Canadian society. Even today, the Main continues to exert a special fascination because of its cosmopolitan character and the exciting atmosphere created by its many businesses, factories, restaurants, and cultural and recreational institutions. The various neighbourhoods that have grown up along this boulevard, such as the Jewish quarter, Chinatown and Little Italy, are now part of a "national historic corridor," comprising a six-kilometre section of the street between the St. Lawrence River and Jean-Talon Street.

Year designated: 1996
Proposed location: two plaques, one at each end of the commemorated section of Saint-Laurent Boulevard, i.e. near the river and at the corner of Jean-Talon Street;
plaques to be erected.

5a Saint-Laurent Boulevard, at the corner of Sherbrooke Street, ca. 1910, Neurdein. McCord Museum of Canadian History, Montréal, MP-0000.816.5.

(5b) Poster showing the diversity and cosmopolitan aspect so characteristic of Saint-Laurent Boulevard. Bernard Pelletier, Parks Canada, Québec, September 2002.

(5c) Saint-Laurent Boulevard, at the corner of Craig (Saint-Antoine) Street, ca. 1895, William Notman & Son. McCord Museum of Canadian History, Montréal, VIEW-2698.

Sir Louis-Hippolyte LaFontaine (1807-1864)

The library of the Bar of Montréal, located in the city's new courthouse, contains a plaque commemorating the career of Sir Louis-Hippolyte LaFontaine, the eminent 19th-century politician and jurist. Fairness and wisdom were the hallmarks of this man's political career. LaFontaine made history in 1842, when, in a gesture of solidarity with his French-Canadian compatriots, he delivered his first speech to the Parliament of the Province of Canada in French. He retired from politics in 1851 to practice law.

Year designated: 1937
Location: plaque erected in the library of the Bar, on the 17th floor of Montréal's courthouse, 10 Saint-Antoine Street East, at the corner of Saint-Laurent Boulevard.

Montréal City Hall

In the 19th century Montréal was the largest urban centre in Canada and the first to build a monumental city hall. This building, which was erected between 1872 and 1878, is typical of Second Empire architecture in Canada. In 1922 a fire largely destroyed the structure, sparing only its outer stone walls. The interior was completely rebuilt, and the new, lavishly decorated building was inaugurated in 1926. Often the theatre of momentous events, Montréal's city hall has played a key role in the city's social and political life. Due to its fascinating past and its undeniable architectural value, this cultural property is one of the most eloquent testaments to the history of Old Montréal and our heritage.

Year designated: 1984
Location: 275 Notre-Dame Street East, at the corner of Gosford; plaque to be erected.

⑥ Sir Louis-Hippolyte LaFontaine, photograph of a portrait, 1905, Albert Ferland. NAC, C-005961.
⑦ Montréal City Hall and Jacques-Cartier Market in 1898. BNQ, Albums E.-Z. Massicotte, Albums de rues, 2-117-a.

Château Ramezay

This building was named Château Ramezay in 1903 in honour of its first owner, Claude de Ramezay, Governor of Montréal. The structure has undergone numerous changes since it was erected in 1705, making it difficult to identify its original architectural features. Among its most famous occupants were the Compagnie des Indes occidentales (1745-1763), a number of governors general (1773-1844) and the Executive Council (in 1839). The museum was established by the Antiquarian and Numismatic Society of Montreal in 1895.

Year designated: 1949
Location: plaque erected to the right of the entrance, 280 Notre-Dame Street East.

⑧ Château Ramezay, ca. 1903.
Postcard, Parks Canada Collection, Quebec Service Centre.

Louis-Joseph Papineau (1786-1871)

This legendary figure is considered the greatest Canadian politician of the first half of the 19th century, as well as the father of French-Canadian nationalism. His election as member for the riding of Kent (Chambly) in 1808 marked the beginning of a long political career that lasted until 1854. Leader of the Canadian Party (Patriot Party as of 1826), he became speaker of the House of Assembly of Lower Canada in 1815. In this capacity, he ardently defended the rights of French Canadians and promoted ministerial accountability. Known for his charisma and eloquence, Papineau was the guiding spirit of the Rebellion of 1837-1838, whose failure forced him into exile, first to the United States and then to France, where he lived until 1845. He returned to Canadian politics in 1848, but played a somewhat secondary role, taking more of an interest in running his seigneury of Petite-Nation. He died at his manor in Montebello at the age of 85. To this day, the French expression "la tête à Papineau" (the mind of a Papineau) designates a very intelligent person.

Year designated: 1937
Proposed location: 440 Bonsecours Street;
plaque to be erected.

Maison Cartier

The Maison Cartier was built following a land speculation deal made at a time when low-cost temporary housing was in high demand. Erected in Place Jacques-Cartier in 1812 and 1813, it illustrates, through its building materials, proportions, roof and firewalls, a type of urban architecture found in Quebec in the early 19th century. Used as a house, inn or tavern for most of its existence, it was occupied until recently by a restaurant.

Year designated: 1982
Location: 407-413 Place Jacques-Cartier, next to the Nelson Hotel;
plaque to be erected.

⑨ Louis-Joseph Papineau in 1832, by R. A. Sproule.
NAC, C-005462.

⑪ Maison Cartier (centre), Place Jacques-Cartier, mid 19th century.
Parks Canada Collection, Quebec Service Centre.

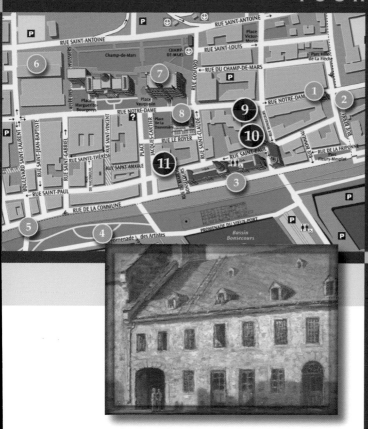

Maison Papineau

This house on Bonsecours Street was built in 1785 by Colonel John Campbell, the Indian Commissioner in the district of Montréal. In 1809 Campbell's widow sold the house to Joseph Papineau, and in 1814 the latter gave it to his famous son Louis-Joseph, who then lived here on a somewhat irregular basis. Work that Louis-Joseph did on the building as of 1831 changed its appearance considerably, both inside and out. Among other things, he extended the house to the next building, built a carriage entrance and raised the façade, covering it with imitation-ashlar wood sheathing. Subsequently, the building served a number of different functions and was even a hotel at one time. The journalist Eric McLean bought the property in 1961 and spent several years restoring it to the way it looked in Papineau's day. McLean, who passed away recently, is generally thought of as a pioneer, since his work gave a definite impetus to the movement for the protection and presentation of Old Montréal.

Year designated: 1968
Location: 440 Bonsecours Street;
plaque to be erected.

 Maison Papineau, as painted by Georges Delfosse ca. 1937.
Ville de Montréal. Gestion de documents et archives. A-656-7.

OLD MONTRÉAL

⑫

The Origins of Montréal

Pointe-à-Callière, which was known to aboriginal people for centuries before Europeans ever set foot there, is the birthplace of Montréal. Maisonneuve founded Ville-Marie on this spot in 1642, and the following year, he built a fort here. Around 1688 Louis-Hector de Callière, the third governor of the city, had a house on this site, hence the name Pointe-à-Callière. In addition to witnessing the birth of Montréal, this spot saw the transformation of the city into one of the largest urban centres in Canada. The Montréal Museum of Archaeology and History, erected on the site, recounts this fascinating story.

Year designated: 1924
Location: plaque erected at the Montréal Museum of Archaeology and History, Pointe-à-Callière, 350 Place Royale.

Great Peace of Montréal

⑬

A peace conference held in Montréal in the summer of 1701 brought together 1,300 Aboriginal chiefs, ambassadors and delegates, as well as a number of colonial dignitaries, including Governor Louis-Hector de Callière. A treaty was ratified on August 4 by representatives of New France, the Iroquois League of Five Nations (excluding the Mohawks) and over 30 other First Nations allied with the French. This treaty put an end to a century of conflict and brought peace to a vast area extending from Acadia to Lake Superior and from the Ottawa River to the confluence of the Mississippi and Missouri. The Treaty of Montréal had a profound and lasting impact on relations among First Nations people, and its terms were still invoked in 1798.

Year designated: 2000
Proposed location: Place de la Grande-Paix, near the Montréal Museum of Archaeology and History, Pointe-à-Callière, 350 Place Royale; plaque to be erected.

⑫ Bas-relief on the monument to Maisonneuve in Place d'Armes, depicting the founding of Ville-Marie, 1895, Louis-Philippe Hébert. Photo: Rémi Chénier, Parks Canada, Québec, November 2002.
⑬ Stamp commemorating the Great Peace of Montréal, issued on August 3, 2001.
"© Canada Post Corporation, 2001. Reproduced with permission."

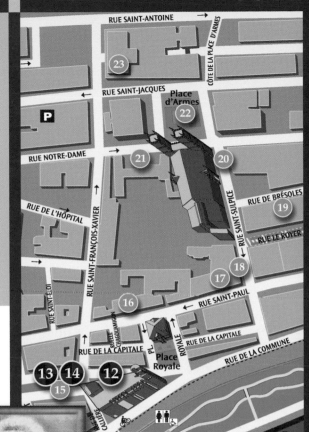

Louis-Hector de Callière (1648-1703)

(14)

Callière was born in Normandy on November 12, 1648. After joining the army around 1664, he took part in several campaigns launched by Louis XIV. In 1684, he was appointed governor of Montréal. Extremely intelligent, he proved a very skilled negotiator with the Amerindians. After being named governor general of New France in September 1699, he was entrusted with the task of establishing a lasting peace among three groups: the Iroquois, the Amerindian nations who were allied with the French, and the colony. Along with Kondiaronk, Callière was one of the main architects of the general peace of 1701. He died in Québec City on May 26, 1703, as a result of an internal hemorrhage. Many delegates from the various Amerindian nations came to Montréal to mourn his loss and renew their allegiance to the 1701 treaty. According to one of Callière's biographers, "there probably never was, in the history of the colony, an abler or more devoted servant of the French monarchy."

OLD MONTRÉAL

Year designated: 2000

Proposed location: Place de la Grande-Paix, near the Montréal Museum of Archaeology and History, Pointe-à-Callière, 350 Place Royale; plaque to be erected.

(14) **Louis-Hector de Callière.**
ANQQ, Livernois, n.d., P560, S2, P166085.

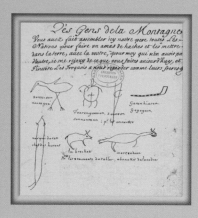

Kondiaronk (ca. 1625-1701)

Chief of the Wyandots of Michilimakinac, Kondiaronk (nicknamed *le Rat* by the French) is considered the principal architect of the Treaty of Montréal. It was thanks to him that so many Aboriginal nations took part in the talks of July 1701, and his skill as a diplomat and orator was vital to the signing of the treaty. On August 1, 1701, although suffering from a very high fever, Kondiaronk delivered a speech that proved crucial to the future of the peace settlement. Shortly afterwards, he was taken to the hospital in Montréal, where he died the next morning. His funeral, which was grandiose, was held on August 3, and he was buried in the city's church. Although his grave is no longer visible today, it is believed to lie somewhere beneath Place d'Armes or in the immediate vicinity.

Year designated: 2000
Proposed location: Place de la Grande-Paix, near the Montréal Museum of Archaeology and History, Pointe-à-Callière, 350 Place Royale;
plaque to be erected.

The Old Custom House

This Palladian-style building, situated near the river, on what has been the busiest spot in Old Montréal since the 17th century, is a prestigious monument to the city's commercial and port activities. It housed the Customs Service until 1871. Despite extensive enlargements to the structure in 1881 and 1882, its exterior has retained a harmonious appearance. Since 1992 the Old Custom House has been part of the Montréal Museum of Archaeology and History.

Year designated: 1997
Location: 150 Saint-Paul Street West;
plaque to be erected.

(15) Signature of *le Rat*, Kondiaronk, at the lower left-hand corner of the 1701 peace treaty.
Reproduced from AN, AC, C11A, vol. 19, fol. 43.
(16) Custom House in 1886, George Charles Arless.
McCord Museum of Canadian History, Montréal, MP-0000.236.4.

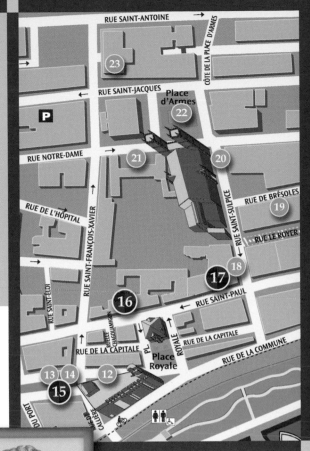

Jean-Baptiste Le Moyne de Bienville (1680-1767)

17

Born in Montréal in 1680, Jean-Baptiste Le Moyne de Bienville belonged to a family that had quite an impact on Canada's history. Bienville became a midshipman in 1692 and served alongside his older brother, Pierre Le Moyne d'Iberville, during several military expeditions, particularly on the Mississippi River. In 1701 he was named commander of Fort Biloxi, and, on four separate occasions between 1701 and 1742, he served as governor of Louisiana. Jean-Baptiste Le Moyne de Bienville founded the cities of Mobile, Alabama, and New Orleans in the course of his career, and a splendid statue has been erected in his honour in the latter city. He made Louisiana a centre of French culture in America. Known as "the father of Louisiana," he died in Paris in 1767.

OLD MONTRÉAL

Year designated: 1953
Proposed location: on the site of the house where he was born, 402-404 Saint-Sulpice Street, at the corner of Saint-Paul Street West; plaque to be erected.

17 Jean-Baptiste Le Moyne de Bienville. Portrait published in Benjamin Sulte, *Histoire des Canadiens-Français, 1608-1880* (Montréal: Wilson & Cie), 1882-1884, tome 5.

Pierre Le Moyne, Sieur d'Iberville (1661-1706)

Soldier, ship's captain, explorer and trader, Iberville is one of the most famous sons of New France. Between 1682 and 1697 he distinguished himself in a number of military campaigns aimed at driving the British out of the lucrative fur trade in Hudson Bay. He took part in many successful raids in Acadia and Newfoundland, as well as against British posts on the Atlantic seaboard. Impressed by his exploits, the authorities entrusted him with the mission of finding the mouth of the Mississippi and establishing permanent posts there. Iberville died in Havana in 1706, after conducting a campaign of harassment against British settlements in the West Indies.

Year designated: 1936
Location: plaque erected on the building at 402-404 Saint-Sulpice Street, at the corner of Saint-Paul Street West.

Jeanne Mance (1606-1673)

The Hôtel-Dieu de Montréal, a hospital built around 1645, is one of the greatest achievements of Jeanne Mance, also known as the "angel of the colony." Equally outstanding is the contribution she made as co-founder of Montréal. Owing to her talent for organization and diplomacy, she saved the colony from financial ruin and Iroquois raids on numerous occasions. Founder, administrator and "nurse-doctor" of the Hôtel-Dieu, she cared for the sick and the wounded in this hospital. Jeanne Mance is considered the "first lay nurse in Canada."

Year designated: 1998
Proposed location: Le Cours le Royer, between Saint-Sulpice and Saint-Didier streets; plaque to be erected.

(18) Pierre Le Moyne d'Iberville, etching by Frédéric Auguste La Guillermie (1841-1934). NAC, C-001349.
(19) Jeanne Mance, by Dugardin, second half of the 19th century. Collection of the Religious Hospitallers of St. Joseph in Montréal, 984X618.

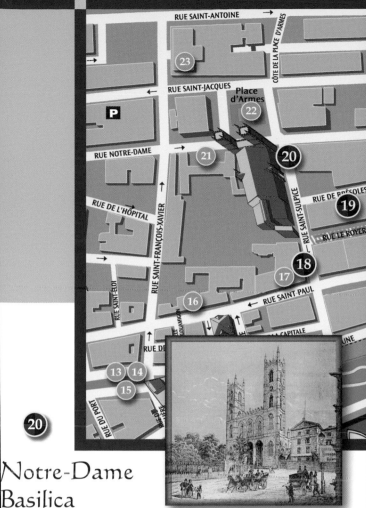

Notre-Dame Basilica

No doubt the most important landmark in Old Montréal, this church is situated in the heart of a religious complex that also comprises a museum, a presbytery, a chapel and a sacristy. It replaced Montréal's first real church, completed in 1683. A masterpiece of Canadian Gothic Revival architecture, Notre-Dame was built between 1824 and 1829 by James O'Donnell, an architect of Irish origin. On O'Donnell's death, the work was pursued by John Ostell. Ostell erected two towers on the façade of the building, in accordance with his predecessor's plans. The west tower, *La Persévérance*, was finished in 1841, and the east one, *La Tempérance*, in 1843. The church's magnificent interior decor, which is renowned worldwide, was designed by Victor Bourgeau and completed between 1872 and 1884. The Sacré-Cœur Chapel (1888-1891) is the work of architects Perrault and Mesnard. Ravaged by fire in 1978, it was restored between 1979 and 1982. Notre-Dame Church was raised to the rank of a minor basilica by Pope John Paul II on April 21, 1982.

Year designated: 1989
Location: 116 Notre-Dame Street West;
plaque to be erected.

(20) Notre-Dame Church, Montréal, May 1870, William Augustus Leggo et Cie.
BNQ, *L'Opinion publique*, vol. 1, no. 19, p. 149 (May 12, 1870).

Sulpician Seminary Gardens

The Sulpician Seminary Gardens, located in the heart of the city, date back to the mid 17th century. In keeping with monastic tradition, the Sulpicians laid out this space next to their seminary for the purpose of meditating and growing fruits and vegetables. The geometric arrangement of the pathways, alternating with grass and converging on a central statue, borrows elements from French and Sulpician traditions of the Renaissance. These gardens, a rare vestige of the French colonial period in Montréal, are among the oldest of their type in Canada.

Year designated: 1981
Proposed location: Sulpician Seminary, 116 Notre-Dame Street West; plaque to be erected.

Paul de Chomedey de Maisonneuve (1612-1676)

Maisonneuve was born near Troyes, in the Champagne region of France, in February 1612. On May 17, 1642, under the aegis of the pious Société de Notre-Dame de Montréal, he established a missionary colony in Canada and founded Ville-Marie. As the first governor of the Island of Montréal, he fiercely defended the colony's interests until he returned to France definitively in the fall of 1665. He died in Paris in 1676. No authentic portrait of Maisonneuve has survived. The statue erected in his memory in Place d'Armes in 1895 was carved by sculptor Louis-Philippe Hébert.

Year designated: 1985
Location: plaque erected on a stele in Place d'Armes, opposite Notre-Dame Basilica, at 116 Notre-Dame Street West.

(21) Sulpician Seminary Gardens, n.d.
BNQ, Albums E.-Z. Massicotte, Albums de rues, 4-15-c.
(22) Detail of the monument to Paul de Chomedey de Maisonneuve by Louis-Philippe Hébert, 1895. Photo: Raymond Gagnon, Ville de Montréal, VM94-1993-632-67.

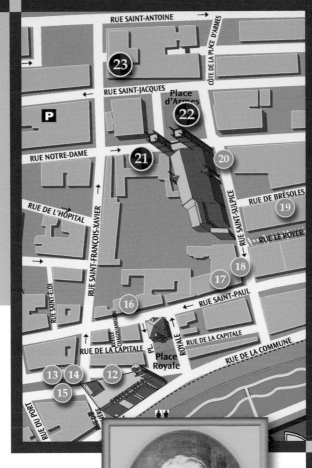

RUE SAINT-ANTOINE

CÔTE DE LA PLACE D'ARMES

23

RUE SAINT-JACQUES

Place d'Armes

22

P

RUE NOTRE-DAME

21

20

RUE DE L'HÔPITAL

RUE SAINT-FRANÇOIS-XAVIER

RUE SAINT-SULPICE

RUE DE BRÉSOLES

19

RUE LE ROYER

18

17

RUE SAINT-É-OI

16

RUE SAINT-PAUL

RUELLE CHAGOUAMIGON

PL. ROYALE

RUE DE LA CAPITALE

13 14

12

RUE DE LA CAPITALE

Place Royale

RUE DE LA COMMUNE

15

RUE DU PORT

Augustin Cuvillier
(1779-1849)

OLD MONTRÉAL

Businessman, militia officer, politician and justice of the peace, Cuvillier distinguished himself mainly in politics and business. A rising star of the Canadian Party in 1828, he was one of the delegates selected to go to London to present the grievances of the Canadian people. Despite his opposition to Papineau and his refusal to sign the latter's *Ninety-two Resolutions*, he became the first speaker of the new House of Assembly following the Act of Union of 1840. This indefatigable worker also co-founded the Bank of Montreal in 1817 and served as president of Montréal's Committee of Trade from 1837 to 1841.

Year designated: 1969
Location: plaque erected near the entrance to
the Bank of Montreal Museum, 129 Saint-Jacques Street West.

23 Augustin (Austin) Cuvillier.
ANQQ, P1000, S4, PC124.

Henri Bourassa (1868-1952)

Best known as the founder of *Le Devoir* in 1910, Henri Bourassa directed this newspaper until 1932. A grandson of Louis-Joseph Papineau, he was born in Montréal on September 1, 1868. In the course of his life, Bourassa fought British imperialism and campaigned for Canadian autonomy and biculturalism. A journalist, politician, pamphleteer and renowned orator, he was also a prolific writer; a bibliography of his works dating from 1966 covers over 87 pages. Henri Bourassa died in Outremont on August 31, 1952.

Year designated: 1962
Location: plaque erected on the building that once housed the offices of *Le Devoir*, 211 Saint-Sacrement Street.

Parliament of the Province of Canada (1844-1849)

Ottawa has not always been the capital of Canada. Indeed, Kingston (1841) and Montréal (1844) had this honour before Ottawa did. In Montréal, Parliament rented premises at Sainte-Anne Market, which occupied a large block east of McGill Street, now known as Place d'Youville. The Parliament Buildings were set ablaze on April 25, 1849, during a riot sparked by Lord Elgin's decision to compensate victims for losses sustained during the Uprisings of 1837-1838. The Legislature sat for the rest of the session in Bonsecours Market. From 1850 to 1865, the seat of government alternated between Toronto and Québec City and in 1866 was finally transferred to Ottawa.

Year designated: 1949
Proposed location: Place d'Youville; plaque to be erected.

(24) Henri Bourassa, July 1917.
NAC, C-009092.
(25) Burning of the Parliament Buildings in Montréal, 1849, C.W. Jefferys.
NAC, C-073717.

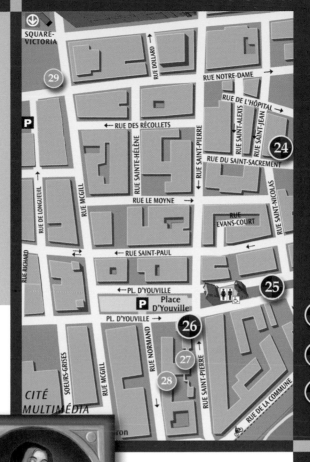

SQUARE-VICTORIA

㉙

P

RUE DOLLARD

RUE NOTRE-DAME

RUE DE L'HÔPITAL

← RUE DES RÉCOLLETS

RUE SAINTE-HÉLÈNE

RUE SAINT-PIERRE

RUE SAINT-ALEXIS

RUE SAINT-JEAN

㉔

RUE DU SAINT-SACREMENT

RUE MCGILL

RUE LE MOYNE →

RUE DE LONGUEUIL

RUE SAINT-NICOLAS

RUE EVANS-COURT

RUE RICHARD

← RUE SAINT-PAUL

←

← PL. D'YOUVILLE

P

Place D'Youville

PL. D'YOUVILLE →

㉕

㉖

SOEURS-GRISES

RUE MCGILL

RUE NORMAND

㉗

RUE SAINT-PIERRE

㉘

CITÉ MULTIMÉDIA

RUE DE LA COMMUNE

㉔
㉕
㉖

㉖

Mother Marie-Marguerite d'Youville (1701-1771)

Born Marie-Marguerite Dufrost de la Jemmerais, this deeply religious woman left her mark on Montréal society through her exemplary piety and her devotion to the poor. Her work continues to this day through the activities of the Sisters of Charity, or Grey Nuns, the community she founded in 1737. In 1747, Marguerite d'Youville took over the administration of the Hôpital général de Montréal from the Charron Brothers, after they abandoned their endeavours. She dedicated herself body and soul to this institution until the day she died.

Year designated: 1973
Location: plaque erected on the building at 138 Saint-Pierre Street, at the corner of Place d'Youville.

㉖ Mother d'Youville, as painted by Antoine Plamondon
after François Malépart de Beaucourt, ca. 1873.
Musée national des beaux-arts du Québec, accession number 56.421.
Photo: Jean-Guy Kérouac.

Grey Nuns of Montréal

This congregation, founded by Marguerite d'Youville in 1737, is one of the oldest religious communities in Canada. Originally dedicated to serving the poor and the helpless, its members eventually worked in health care and education as well, leading to the creation of several separate religious communities in Canada and the United States. In 1844, the Grey Nuns became the first nuns to work in Western Canada.

Year designated: 1988
Proposed location: Maison de Mère d'Youville, 138 Saint-Pierre Street; plaque to be erected.

The Grey Nuns' Hospital

Within these walls, the Grey Nuns cared for Montréal's sick and underprivileged until 1871. They thus followed in the footsteps of the Charron Brothers, who had built an almshouse known as the Hôpital général de Montréal in 1692. This building, with its rough masonry, ashlar details and gable roof, displays a functional type of architecture typical of the 18th century. Enlarged on several occasions in the 19th century, the building was later demolished in part, particularly when Normand and Saint-Pierre streets were opened. One of the wings of the nuns' convent and some of the walls of their chapel on Saint-Pierre Street have survived to this day.

Year designated: 1973
Location: Maison de Mère d'Youville, plaque erected to the right of the secondary entrance near Place d'Youville, 121 Normand Street.

(27) Group of Grey Nuns, 20th century, Chesterfield Inlet, Nunavut.
Grey Nuns' Archives, St. Boniface.
(28) Grey Nuns' Hospital, before 1870.
Parks Canada Collection, Quebec Service Centre.

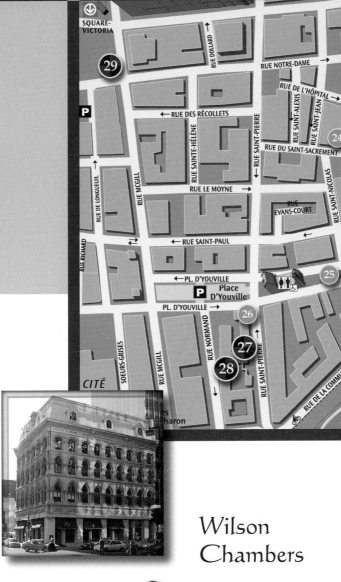

27
28
29

OLD MONTRÉAL

Wilson Chambers

A veritable jewel of Montréal's architectural heritage, Wilson Chambers is one of the few commercial buildings designed in the Gothic Revival style in the city. Its roof in the Second Empire style so popular during the Victorian era adds to the building's interest. This structure was erected in 1868 for Charles Wilson, a politician, trader and former mayor of Montréal. Several well-known businesses have occupied it over the years: O. McGarvey & Son, cabinetmakers; Herman H. Wolff & Co., importers; and C. A. Workman Limited, makers of a famous brand of work clothes. Wilson Chambers, which currently belongs to 5B Immobilier inc., is now known as the Karkouti Building.

Year designated: 1990
Location: Karkouti Building, 502-510 McGill Street, at the corner of Notre-Dame; plaque to be erected.

(29) Wilson Chambers on the corner of McGill Street, as seen from Notre-Dame Street.
Photo: Rémi Chénier, Parks Canada, Québec, November 2002.

DOWNT

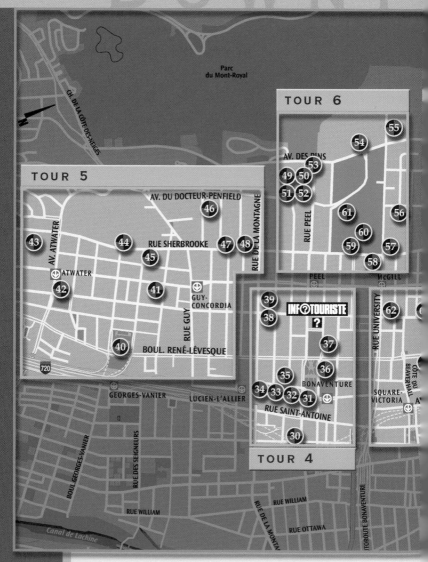

Postal Service

30

During the French Regime, the Intendant sent government dispatches by messenger between Québec City and Montréal, and it was not until 1693 that the first royal courier, Pierre DaSilva, began to carry mail between the two cities. However, delivery was slow, poorly organized and very costly until after the Conquest, when it was taken over by the British. In 1763, two districts were created to administer postal service in Britain's North American colonies. The northern district, which stretched from Québec to Virginia, was entrusted to Hugh Finlay, first postmaster of Québec. In 1764 a regular courier service between Québec City, Montréal and New York was put in place, laying the foundations of Canada's postal service.

Year designated: 1927
Location: plaque erected outside the entrance to the post office, 1015 Saint-Jacques Street West, at the corner of De la Cathédrale.

Windsor Station

31

This superb Romanesque Revival building, which was inaugurated in 1889, served not only as a railway terminal but also as the head office of the Canadian Pacific Railway, one of Canada's leading rail companies. Its presence testifies to Montréal's importance as a rail hub during the late 19th and early 20th centuries. The building still houses the Canadian Pacific Railway's head office, but the station itself is used only for suburban rail traffic. It was designated a heritage railway station in 1990.

Year designated: 1975
Location: 900 Peel Street, at the corner of De La Gauchetière; plaque to be erected.

30 Stamp commemorating the first post road between Québec, Trois-Rivières, Montréal and New York. "© Canada Post Corporation, 1963. Reproduced with permission."
31 CPR's Windsor Station in Montréal.
BNQ, *Le Monde illustré*, vol. 10, no. 481, p. 133 (July 22, 1893).

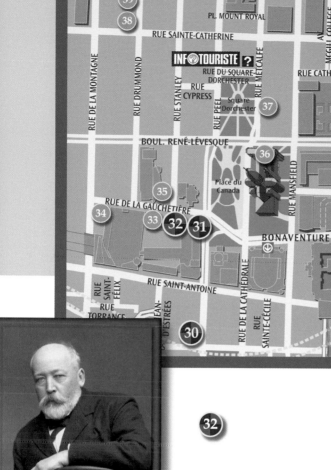

32

Sir William Van Horne (1843-1915)

Railway builder and administrator, collector and artist, William Van Horne was a man with a wide range of talents and interests. He gained national renown for managing the construction of a railroad for the Canadian Pacific Railway, a new company in Canada at the time. Van Horne became general manager of the firm in 1882, vice-president in 1885 and president in 1888. Two years later he had already completed the main portions of the rail system that would contribute so much to the country's development. It was also during his presidency that the Canadian Pacific Railway's head office moved to Windsor Station in Montréal.

Year designated: 1955
Location: plaque erected in the entrance to Windsor Station, 1160 De La Gauchetière Street West, at the corner of Peel.

32 Sir William Van Horne, ca. 1900-1910, William Cooper.
NAC, PA-182603.

DOWNTOWN

Railway Porters and their Unions

Railway porters scored a number of resounding victories for Canada's labour movement. Through their efforts, for example, Blacks won the right to union representation in 1919. However, of even greater significance for the history of human rights in this country, porters and their unions put an end to discrimination in railroad employment in the mid 1950s, thereby setting a precedent whose repercussions were felt well beyond the railway industry.

Year designated: 1994
Location: plaque erected at Windsor Station, 900 Peel Street, at the corner of Saint-Antoine.

Howie Morenz (1902-1937)

Considered the most popular hockey player of the first half of the 20th century, Howie Morenz played with the National Hockey League for 14 seasons, including 11 with the Montreal Canadiens, who recruited him in 1923. The team's star player, he was twice named top scorer of the year and won the Hart Trophy for most valuable player three times. Morenz met with a tragic end, dying as a result of injuries sustained during a match at the Montreal Forum. A true sports legend, he was inducted into the Hockey Hall of Fame in 1945.

Year designated: 1976
Located: plaque erected in the Bell Centre, 1260 De La Gauchetière Street West, at the corner of De la Montagne.

33 Railway porters, union members and members of the Canadian Pacific Railway, ca 1950
Private collection.
34 Howie Morenz.
Photo: James Rice/Hockey Hall of Fame.

DOWNTOWN

St. George's Anglican Church

This Gothic Revival church was built in 1869 and 1870 according to the plans of William T. Thomas. Its most distinctive features are its magnificent beam ceiling, one of the largest of its type in the world, and its interior, which has no columns and uses Gothic architectural motifs in conjunction with a clever combination of visual effects. Its omnipresent wooden features and many splendid stained-glass windows add to the warmth and dignity of the decor.

Year designated: 1990
Location: plaque erected at 1101 Stanley Street, at the corner of De La Gauchetière.

35 St. George's Church, 1881 (copied ca. 1910). McCord Museum of Canadian History, Montréal, MP-0000.849.2.

Marie-Reine-du-Monde Basilica-Cathedral

This basilica-cathedral was modelled on St. Peter's Basilica in Rome at the express request of Mgr. Bourget, the second bishop of Montréal. According to Mgr. Bourget, this symbolic gesture would underscore the attachment of his diocese to the values of Catholicism and the papacy. Known in English as Mary Queen of the World, the Baroque-Revival-style church was built between 1870 and 1894, after the plans of Victor Bourgeau and Father Joseph Michaud. Even though this building is smaller than its famous model, several of its features are evocative of the basilica in Rome: its large dome, interior layout and façade surmounted by 13 statues, as well as its Baroque baldachin, side chapels and the decoration of the vaulted ceiling.

Year designated: 1999
Location: 1085 De la Cathédrale Street, at the corner of René-Lévesque Boulevard; plaque to be erected.

Marie-Reine-du-Monde Basilica-Cathedral, March 26, 1936.
Ville de Montréal. Gestion de documents et archives. VM94-Z175.

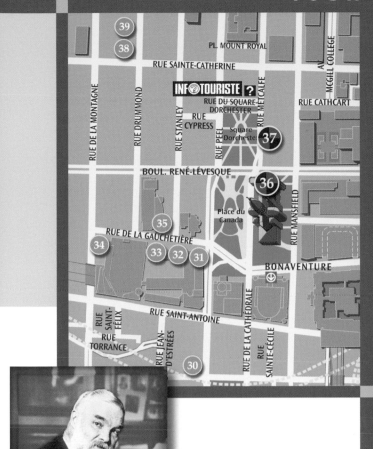

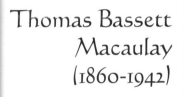

Thomas Bassett
Macaulay
(1860-1942)

Around 1908, Thomas Bassett Macaulay, an actuary and leading Canadian businessman, raised Sun Life, a small Montréal firm, to the rank of one of the most important life insurance companies in the world. After becoming president of Sun Life in 1915, he contributed significantly to Canada's development by reinvesting a large portion of his firm's capital in business initiatives in both the public and industrial sectors. Fascinated by animal breeding and farming, he also contributed to Canada's dairy industry by creating a new strain of Holstein cattle.

Year designated: 1997
Proposed location: Sun Life Building, 1155 Metcalfe Street; plaque to be erected.

(37) Thomas Bassett Macaulay, third president of the Sun Life Assurance Company of Canada.
Sun Life Corporate Archives, I-9800.

Sir George Stephen (1829-1921)

George Stephen played a major role in Canada's development. Of Scottish origin, he came to the colony in 1850 as a general merchant. He soon carved out an enviable place for himself in the business world and in 1876 became president of the Bank of Montreal. Aware of how important communications were to the country's economic growth, Stephen co-founded the Canadian Pacific Railway Company and was instrumental in building the rail system. In recognition of his efforts, the Canadian government awarded him the Medal of the Confederation of Canada in 1885. After returning to England in 1890, he acted as British affairs advisor to Canadian Prime Minister John A. Macdonald. In 1891 Queen Victoria made him Baron Mount Stephen.

Year designated: 1971
Location: plaque erected on the Mount Stephen Club, 1440 Drummond Street.

38 **Lord Mount Stephen, 1829-1921.**
Canadian Pacific Railway Archives, NS.30245.

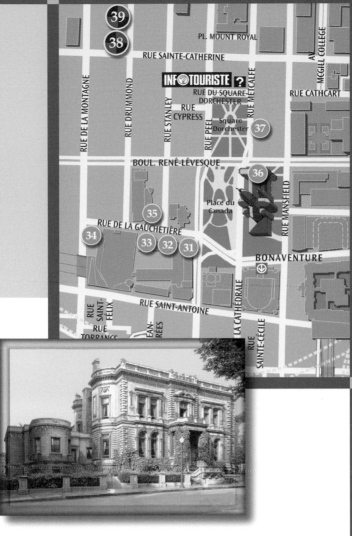

PL. MOUNT ROYAL

RUE SAINTE-CATHERINE

INF@TOURISTE ?

RUE DU SQUARE DORCHESTER

RUE CYPRESS

Square Dorchester

BOUL. RENÉ-LÉVESQUE

Place du Canada

RUE DE LA GAUCHETIÈRE

BONAVENTURE

RUE SAINT-ANTOINE

RUE DE LA MONTAGNE · RUE DRUMMOND · RUE STANLEY · RUE PEEL · RUE METCALFE · RUE CATHCART · MCGILL COLLEGE · RUE MANSFIELD · LA CATHEDRALE · RUE SAINTE-CÉCILE · RUE SAINT-FÉLIX · RUE JEAN-RÉES · RUE TORRANCE

39 38 37 36 35 34 33 32 31

 George Stephen House

This magnificent house of Renaissance inspiration was built in 1880 for George Stephen, president of both the Bank of Montreal and the Canadian Pacific Railway. The building's plans were drawn by English architect W. T. Thomas, while the actual construction was carried out by Montréal contractor J. H. Hutchison. Most of the beautiful construction materials were imported from abroad. It took three years for numerous craftsmen brought especially from Europe to complete the interior decoration of this splendid Victorian building. Estimated to be worth nearly $1 million today, this decor constitutes a unique masterpiece in North America. The George Stephen House has been the property of the Mount Stephen Club since 1926.

Year designated: 1971
Location: plaque erected at the Mount Stephen Club, 1440 Drummond Street.

39 George Stephen House in 1934-1935, William Notman & Son. McCord Museum of Canadian History, Montréal, VIEW-25493.

Van Horne-Shaughnessy House

This magnificent residence stands on part of the property that formerly belonged to the Sulpicians, who founded a mission at this spot in 1676. One of the few double houses of Second Empire inspiration in Montréal, it was built to the plans of W. T. Thomas in 1874 and evokes the time when René-Lévesque Boulevard was lined with large mansions surrounded by landscaped gardens. This house has been owned and occupied by several famous people, including Duncan McIntyre, William Van Horne and T. G. Shaughnessy, three key figures in the Canadian Pacific Railway. Purchased by Montréal architect Phyllis Lambert in 1974, this structure was extensively restored to incorporate it into the Canadian Centre for Architecture, inaugurated in 1989.

Year designated: 1973
Location: plaque set in the wall surrounding the house, 1923 René-Lévesque Boulevard West, near Saint-Marc.

Royal Montreal Curling Club

According to some sources, the first curling match in North America was played by Scottish members of the British army when it occupied Québec City in the winter of 1759-1760. Whatever the case may be, the sport was well established by January 1807, when the first duly constituted curling club was founded on the continent: the Montreal Curling Club. Its first 20 members played on the frozen surface of the St. Lawrence River using "stones" made of cast iron, as no granite ones were available. During the early years members also played on the frozen waters of the Lachine Canal basin, streams and lakes, and even on the ice that formed on the flooded floors of abandoned warehouses. In 1889 the club built a curling shed with three playing areas, or "rinks," and, three years later it erected a clubhouse after the plans of architect A. T. Taylor. Nobbs and Hyde enlarged the latter building in 1929. The Royal (added in 1924) Montreal Curling Club testifies not only to the city's leading role in the development of sports in Canada, but also, through the assembly and span of its curling shed's roof trusses, to advances in engineering in this country.

Year designated: 1953
Location: plaque erected in the entrance hall, 1850 De Maisonneuve Boulevard West.

40 Van Horne-Shaughnessy House, ca. 1880.
McCord Museum of Canadian History, Montréal, MP-1981.207.13.
41 Curling match on the St. Lawrence River in 1855, W.S. Hatton.
NAC, C-040148.

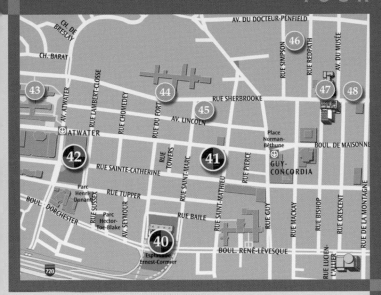

Montreal Forum

Built in 1924, the Montreal Forum was for many years the most renowned sports facility in Canada. Home for over 70 years to the famous Montreal Canadiens Hockey Club, it symbolized our national sport. The building was not only used for hockey games, but also served as a venue for numerous cultural, political and religious events throughout its history. Purchased by Canderel in 1998, it has been converted into a large entertainment complex housing movie theatres, stores, restaurants and a museum devoted to the "legends of the Forum."

Year designated: 1997
Location: Pepsi Forum Entertainment Centre, 2313 Sainte-Catherine Street West, at the corner of Atwater; plaque to be erected.

DOWNTOWN

The Forum in April 1947, National Film Board of Canada.
NAC, PA-129603.

Congrégation de Notre-Dame

The Congrégation de Notre-Dame, founded by Marguerite Bourgeoys in 1658, was the first uncloistered religious community in New France. For over 300 years, these nuns have pursued the work of their founder, mainly by providing elementary, secondary and college education around the world. Their ministry also includes various social services, pastoral activities and volunteer work. The congregation's motherhouse used to be located on the grounds of the Villa Maria Convent, which was purchased by the nuns in 1854.

Year designated: 1988
Proposed location: Dawson College (former motherhouse of the Congrégation de Notre-Dame), 2330 Sherbrooke Street West; plaque to be erected.

Sulpician Towers (Fort de la Montagne)

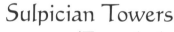
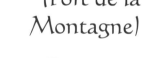
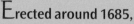

Erected around 1685, both of these towers were once part of a fort built by the Sulpicians to protect their Amerindian mission. Although a fire broke out in the fort in 1694, the towers were spared, and the mission's nuns are believed to have obtained permission at this time to live in the east tower and use the west one as a school. In 1825 the Sulpicians converted the east tower into a chapel and continued to use it as such until 1930. Apart from these two towers, all traces of the fort disappeared when the seminary was built around 1855. These twin towers are among the oldest buildings on the Island of Montréal. Restored between 1984 and 1986, they have retained their main original features.

Year designated: 1970
Location: 2065 Sherbrooke Street West, opposite Du Fort; plaque to be erected.

(43) Community garden, Congrégation de Notre-Dame, ca. 1885, Oliver B. Buell. McCord Museum of Canadian History, Montréal, MP-0000.2924.
(44) Site of the Fort de la Montagne / Collège de Montréal, Sherbrooke Street, 1891. BNQ, Albums E.-Z. Massicotte, Albums de rues, 8-80-a.

 Montreal Masonic Memorial Temple

DOWNTOWN

Built in 1929-1930, this magnificent building on Sherbrooke Street West is one of the finest examples of the Beaux-Arts style in Canada. Its architecture, inspired by Greek temples of antiquity, clearly reflects the aspirations of its owners, the Freemasons. The ornamental elements on its façade are symbolic representations of Freemasons' beliefs, while the tripartite division of the façade evokes both the various stages of life and the three levels in the fraternity's hierarchy. The four large Ionic columns are intended as an allegory of divine wisdom. The Montreal Masonic Memorial Temple is one of the last surviving Masonic temples in Canada.

Year designated: 2001
Location: 1850 Sherbrooke Street West,
at the corner of Saint-Marc; plaque to be erected.

Façade of the Montreal Masonic Memorial Temple.
Photo: Rémi Chénier, Parks Canada, Québec, November 2003.

73

John Rose
(1820-1888)

Lawyer, financier, politician and diplomat, John Rose distinguished himself as finance minister of Canada's first Parliament. From 1867 to 1869, he worked on the adoption of the Dominion's first banking system, helped to negotiate a loan for building the Intercontinental Railway and took part in a number of talks with the Government of the United States. Even after he left politics, he was called upon to use his diplomatic skills to improve British-U.S. relations in the wake of the Civil War. A highly influential man, Rose received the Prince of Wales at his home in Montréal when the Prince was on an official visit to North America.

Year designated: 1973
Proposed location: Simpson Street, at the spot where John Rose's house used to stand; plaque to be erected.

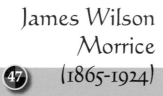

James Wilson Morrice
(1865-1924)

Morrice, who was born in Montréal, was one of the most famous landscape painters of his day. Following in the footsteps of the Impressionists, he strove to capture the changing effects of light on architecture and on the landscape, particularly on or near water. An extensive traveller, he took part in many international exhibitions. Morrice won a very enviable reputation in the course of his successful career, not only in Canada but also France, his country of adoption. Two of his paintings, *The Ferry, Quebec* and *Ice Bridge at Quebec*, are among his first major Canadian works.

Year designated: 1954
Location: plaque erected in the Hornstein Pavilion, Montreal Museum of Fine Arts, 1379 Sherbrooke Street West.

46 The Honourable John Rose, 1868, William Notman.
McCord Museum of Canadian History, Montréal, I-33888.
47 James Wilson Morrice, 1900, William Notman & Son.
McCord Museum of Canadian History, Montréal, II-132335.

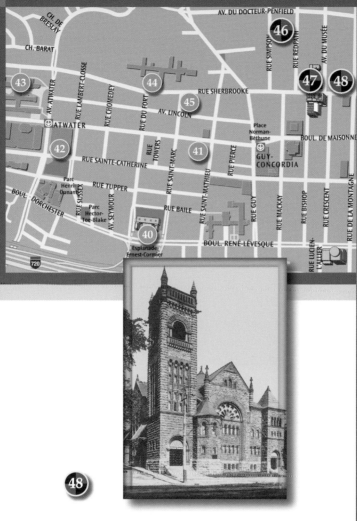

Erskine and American United Church

Built in 1893-1894, the Erskine and American United Church is a magnificent example of the Romanesque Revival style, inspired by the work of American architect H. H. Richardson. The most distinctive features of its exterior, which looks almost exactly as it did when the church was first erected, are the attractive masonry and the three-tiered arrangement of windows of varied form and design. The interior layout is an interesting combination of the building's original amphitheatre plan and changes made by Percy Nobbs in 1938-1939 in response to new standards set by the United Church. This church has one of Canada's largest collections of religious stained glass by the celebrated American artist L. C. Tiffany.

Year designated: 1998
Location: 1339 Sherbrooke Street West,
at the corner of Du Musée Avenue; plaque to be erected.

DOWNTOWN

48 Erskine and American United Church, ca. 1910, Neurdein.
McCord Museum of Canadian History, Montréal, MP-0000.872.7.

Maude Elizabeth Seymour Abbott (1869-1940)

McGill University's Faculty of Medicine can be proud that one of the first woman doctors in Canada was a member of its staff. Maude Abbott was a pioneer in the field of medical research and education, and her work and many writings on congenital heart disease won her international acclaim. Founder of the university's medical museum, she disseminated her expertise worldwide. This forward-looking woman helped to facilitate access for women to higher education, particularly in medicine, which had thus far been the exclusive preserve of men.

Year designated: 1993
Location: plaque erected at McGill University, McIntyre Medical Sciences Building, 3655 Promenade Sir-William-Osler.

Edward William Archibald (1872-1945)

After graduating from McGill University in 1896, Archibald enjoyed a long and brilliant career as a surgeon at Montréal's Royal Victoria Hospital. As he suffered from tuberculosis, he took a special interest in this terrible disease and was eventually recognized as one of the best thoracic surgeons of the 1920s and 1930s. His contribution to neurosurgery is also worthy of mention. A prolific author and speaker, this world-renowned specialist was elected president of the American Surgical Association in 1935.

Year designated: 1998
Proposed location: McGill University, McIntyre Medical Sciences Building, 3655 Promenade Sir-William-Osler; plaque to be erected.

(49) Maude Abbott in 1887, William Notman & Son.
McCord Museum of Canadian History, Montréal, II-85442.
(50) Dr. Edward William Archibald, professor of surgery at McGill and first neurosurgeon in Canada. McGill University, Wilder Penfield Archive.

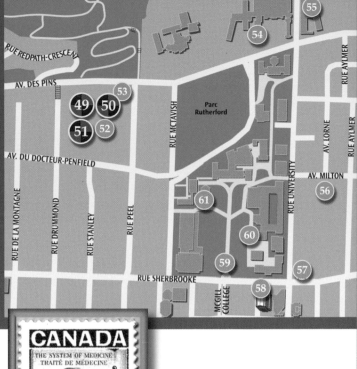

Sir William Osler (1849-1919)

William Osler was one of the leaders in Canada's medical field in the late 19th century. After studying at McGill University and in Europe, he embarked on a brilliant career in medical education and clinical medicine at McGill. As of 1876 he worked as a pathologist at the Montreal General Hospital, and in 1889 he became a professor of medicine at Johns Hopkins University and physician-in-chief at the hospital affiliated with this institution. In 1905 he was appointed *Regius Professor of Medicine* at Oxford University. William Osler published numerous books, including *The Principles and Practice of Medicine*, the most famous and most re-edited medical textbook of the 20th century. Osler contributed greatly to the shape of modern medicine.

Year designated: 1982
Location: plaque erected at McGill University, McIntyre Medical Sciences Building, 3655 Promenade Sir-William-Osler.

Margaret Ridley Charlton
(1858-1931)

52

Margaret Ridley Charlton was born in Laprairie, near Montréal. In 1895 she became assistant librarian at McGill University's medical library, which she changed radically. In 1898, in concert with Drs. William Osler and George Milbray Gould, among others, she founded the Medical Library Association, an international organization that would play a key role in specialized, university-level library science. She left McGill in 1914 to work as a librarian for the Academy of Medicine of the University of Toronto, where she stayed until 1922. Margaret Charlton was a pioneer in that she pursued a career in library science at a time when this field of endeavour was not yet recognized as a profession and most medical librarians were male doctors. As illustrated by her many writings, she was one of the first to take an interest in the history of medicine in Quebec. She also wrote several children's books, including the first book of fairy tales ever published in Canada: *A Wonder Web of Stories*.

Year designated: 2002
Proposed location: Health Sciences Library, McGill University,
3655 Promenade Sir-William-Osler; plaque to be erected.

52 **Margaret Ridley Charlton.**
Osler Library of the History of Medicine, McGill University, Montréal, Quebec.

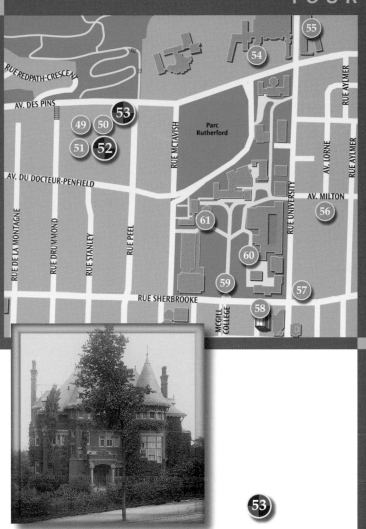

H. Vincent Meredith Residence

This beautiful city house, which looks like a medieval castle, was built in 1896 for Andrew Allan, an associate of the Allan Line Steamship Company and the father-in-law of H. Vincent Meredith, Manager of the Bank of Montreal. Designed by Edward Maxwell in the Queen Anne Revival style, this magnificent residence displays a harmonious combination of classical features (Venetian window and columned porch) and medieval characteristics (tower, ribbed chimneys and steeply pitched roof). Asymmetrical plans are one of the hallmarks of this architectural style.

Year designated: 1990
Location: 1110 des Pins Avenue West, at the corner of Peel; plaque to be erected.

(53) H. V. Meredith Residence in 1906, William Notman & Son. McCord Museum of Canadian History, Montréal, II-160766.

DOWNTOWN

54a

Hersey Pavilion

This pavilion owes its name to Mabel Hersey, who lived in Canada in the early 20th century and helped to spearhead the movement for the professionalization of nursing. Built in 1906, this building served originally as a residence for nursing students. The construction of an addition with classrooms in 1932 reflected a growing trend toward ever more stringent educational and scientific standards in the profession. Therefore, this pavilion is one of the most appropriate places to commemorate the national historic significance of nursing in Canada. The building is currently used mainly for medical research.

Year designated: 1997
Location: Royal Victoria Hospital, 687 des Pins Avenue West; plaque to be erected.

54b

54a Hersey Pavilion.
Photo: Rémi Chénier, Parks Canada, Québec, November 2003.
54b Hersey Pavilion.
Photo: Rémi Chénier, Parks Canada, Québec, November 2003.

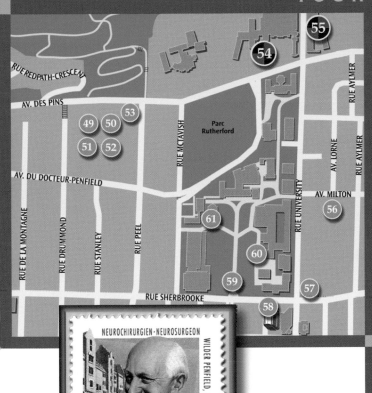

Map with numbered markers. Streets: RUE REDPATH-CRESCENT, AV. DES PINS, AV. DU DOCTEUR-PENFIELD, RUE SHERBROOKE, RUE DE LA MONTAGNE, RUE DRUMMOND, RUE STANLEY, RUE PEEL, RUE MCTAVISH, RUE UNIVERSITY, AV. LORNE, RUE AYLMER, AV. MILTON. Parc Rutherford. Markers: 55, 54, 49, 50, 53, 51, 52, 61, 56, 60, 59, 57, 58.

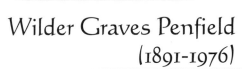

NEUROCHIRURGIEN · NEUROSURGEON
WILDER PENFIELD, 1891-1976
CANADA 40

55

Wilder Graves Penfield
(1891-1976)

Wilder Graves Penfield won international renown for his innovative work in the field of neurosurgery and neurology. A prolific author, he broke new ground with his operating techniques, particularly for epilepsy, and helped to further our knowledge about the functioning of the human brain. Penfield founded the Montreal Neurological Institute in 1934 and served as its director until 1960. This institute is now world-famous for its educational programs, research activities and treatment of diseases related to the brain and the nervous system.

Year designated: 1988
Location: plaque erected on the façade of the Montreal Neurological Institute, 3801 University Street.

DOWNTOWN

Marlborough Apartments

This is one of Montréal's oldest and most beautiful apartment buildings. Designed in the Queen Anne Revival style, it was built in 1900 by architects Andrew Thomas Taylor and George William Gordon for Andrew Frederic Gault. Known as the "cotton king," Gault was president of several textile firms in the Montréal area. This brick building originally had 27 apartments, ranging from bachelor units to nine-room dwellings. Organized around a central courtyard, it was designed like a private residence for "refined" city dwellers. Owned by McGill University from 1960 to 1979, the building was converted into condominiums in the 1990s. A Dutch influence can be detected in the ornamentation of its gables and main façade.

Year designated: 1991
Location: 570 Milton Street, opposite Lorne Avenue; plaque to be erected.

Donald Alexander Smith (1820-1914)

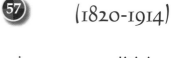

Businessman, politician, diplomat and philanthropist, Donald A. Smith distinguished himself in economic circles as an officer of the Hudson's Bay Company. A principal shareholder of the firm in 1889, he later became its governor. Throughout his life, Smith was active in a multitude of businesses as shareholder, administrator or president. Determined to improve transportation in Canada's northwest, he risked his fortune on building railroads, particularly the Canadian Pacific. Smith's immense wealth was matched only by his generosity, as shown by the more than $7,500,000 in donations and bequests he made over the years. Many Montréal institutions involved in health care, education, sports and the arts were among the beneficiaries. From 1887 to 1896, Smith was member of Parliament for Montreal West and, from 1896 to 1914, high commissioner in London. He was made 1st Baron Strathcona and Mount Royal in 1900.

Year designated: 1974
Proposed location: McGill University, Strathcona Music Building, 555 Sherbrooke Street West, at the corner of University; plaque to be erected.

56 Marlborough Apartments in 1902, William Notman & Son. McCord Museum of Canadian History, Montréal, II-142552.

57 Lord Strathcona driving in the last spike of the Canadian Pacific Railway, 1885, reproduced ca. 1910, Alexander Ross. McCord Museum of Canadian History, Montréal, MP-0000.25.971.

David Ross McCord

(1844-1930)

David Ross McCord was the founder of the McCord Museum of Canadian History. Around 1878, while still a young collector, he decided to start adding his own acquisitions to his family's assets. For this purpose, he invested time and money scouring the country for beautiful objects associated with the history of Canadians. McCord cherished the dream of building a national history museum in Montréal, and in 1919 he bequeathed his personal collection to McGill University. The McCord National Museum opened on Sherbrooke Street on October 13, 1921. Now known as the McCord Museum of Canadian History, this institution continues to pursue its initial mission of making history accessible to all.

Year designated: 1999
Proposed location: McCord Museum, 690 Sherbrooke Street West, at the corner of Victoria; plaque to be erected.

58 David Ross McCord, ca. 1915.
McCord Museum of Canadian History, Montréal, MP-0000.2135.7.

Hochelaga

The fortified village of Hochelaga, visited by Jacques Cartier in 1535, was probably situated near what is now the campus of McGill University. This Iroquoian village was surrounded by a bark-lined palisade and contained dwellings known as "longhouses," which could lodge several members of the same family or clan. The lifespan of such villages was 10 to 25 years, after which they were moved to another location where game and firewood were more abundant and the soil more fertile. This is perhaps why Hochelaga was abandoned around 1600.

Year designated: 1921
Location: plaque erected to the left of the main entrance to McGill University, 845 Sherbrooke Street West.

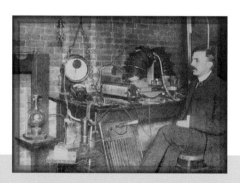

Ernest Rutherford (1871-1937)

Rutherford was a pioneer in nuclear physics research. A physics professor at McGill from 1898 to 1907, he discovered and named alpha rays, beta rays and gamma rays, three of the main components of radiation. In 1919 he successfully completed the first artificial alteration of an atomic structure and thus paved the way for many other researchers. An international authority in his field, Rutherford received the highest honours during his career, including the Nobel Prize in Chemistry in 1908 and the presidency of the Royal Society of London from 1925 to 1929. He was made baron in 1931. His main writings include *Radioactivity* (1904), *Radiation from Radioactive Substances* (1930) and *The Newer Alchimy* (1937). Rutherford's effigy appears on stamps and paper money issued by his homeland, New Zealand.

Year designated: 1939
Location: McGill University, plaque erected on the wall of the MacDonald-Stewart Library, 809 Sherbrooke Street West.

(59) Hypothetical plan of Hochelaga drawn by Ramusio, 1563-1583. NAC, C-010489.
(60) Ernest Rutherford in his laboratory at McGill University, ca. 1905. McCord Museum of Canadian History, Montréal, MP-0000.77.

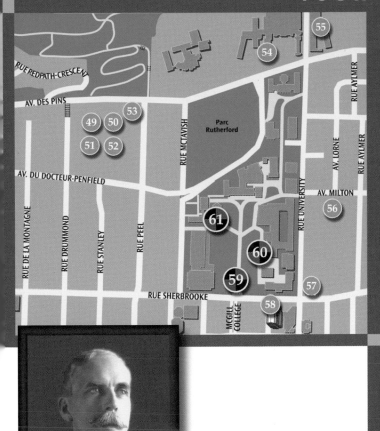

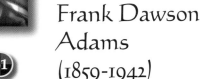

Frank Dawson Adams (1859-1942)

DOWNTOWN

Adams, a world-renowned geologist, studied at McGill University and the University of Heidelberg in Germany. He held a number of positions at McGill during his brilliant career: geology professor, dean of the Faculty of Applied Science and vice-principal. He was also a member of the Geological Society of Canada. His work on the flow of brittle rocks had such a profound impact on the field of geology that he is considered the founder of modern structural geology. A new mineral type discovered on Mount Saint-Hilaire was named adamsite in his honour. Frank Dawson Adams wrote many scientific works, including *The Birth and Development of the Geological Sciences*, published 16 years after he retired.

Year designated: 1950
Location: McGill University, plaque erected to the right of the entrance to the Redpath Museum, 859 Sherbrooke Street West.

Christ Church Cathedral

This Anglican Cathedral in the Gothic Revival style was built between 1857 and 1860 after the plans of Frank Wills and Thomas Seaton Scott. Inspired by cruciform English churches of the 14th century, it illustrates a new architectural and spiritual trend advocated by the Cambridge Camden Society, a group of English theologians. The interior is designed so as to draw attention to the choir and the raised altar, two important features of the new Anglican liturgy in the mid 19th century. Despite the changes this church has undergone over the years, it still retains much of its original plan.

Year designated: 1999
Location: 1444 Union Street, at the corner of Sainte-Catherine; plaque to be erected.

(62) **Christ Church Cathedral in 1868, William Notman.**
McCord Museum of Canadian History, Montréal, I-32441.1.

St. James United Church

When this church opened in 1889, it was the largest Methodist church in the world. After 1925, when the Methodist and various other churches merged to form the United Church of Canada, St. James United Church became a rallying point for the different Protestant denominations in Montréal. This imposing religious monument of High Victorian Gothic Revival inspiration was built to the plans of Alexander F. Dunlop in 1887-1888. The exterior borrows elements from French and Italian architecture, while the interior boasts several very distinctive features, such as the series of inverted arches in the vaulted ceiling, which is unique in Quebec, and the nave, which resembles an amphitheatre. This layout was chosen to satisfy certain requirements stemming from the Methodist liturgy of the word.

DOWNTOWN

Year designated: 1996
Location: plaque erected at 463 Sainte-Catherine Street West, at the corner of Saint-Alexandre.

The Society of Jesus (the Jesuits)

Since the beginnings of the colony, the Jesuits distinguished themselves through their missionary and apostolic work, especially with Amerindians. The most sought-after teachers in Europe, they founded or administered numerous classical colleges in Canada. They were also renowned for their commitment to social action and preaching, and they provided the impetus for Christian renewal through their retreat and pilgrimage centres and their role in specialized apostolate movements, such as the Catholic Union (1858), the Sacred Heart League (1883) and the Catholic Association of French-Canadian Youth (1904). In addition, the Jesuits were instrumental in the emergence of the Catholic labour movement. Faithful to their founder's motto, "To the greater glory of God," they had a profound impact on many aspects of Canadian history.

Year designated: 1988
Location: plaque erected on a stele, near the Church of Le Gesù, 1202 Bleury Street.

64 Church of Le Gesù and Sainte-Marie College.
BNQ, Albums E.-Z. Massicotte, Albums de rues, 1-73-c.

Saint Patrick's Basilica

Saint Patrick's Basilica, which was built to serve Montréal's Irish community, is the oldest English-language Roman Catholic church in the city. Its inauguration in 1847 coincided with the arrival of a large number of Irish immigrants in North America. An early example of the Gothic Revival style in Canada, this basilica was designed by the architect Pierre-Louis Morin and Father Félix Martin. It is very original in that it marries the simplicity of traditional Quebec architecture with features of French medieval inspiration, creating a highly elegant interior. The interior decor as it appears today is mainly the product of work carried out in the late 19th century.

Year designated: 1990
Location: plaque erected at 454-460 René-Lévesque Boulevard West, at the corner of Saint-Alexandre.

65 St. Patrick's Church, late 19th century.
Archives de l'Université de Montréal, fonds William-Henry Atherton / p0060FC00021.

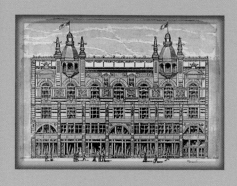

Monument-National

This large building was erected by the Association Saint-Jean-Baptiste de Montréal between 1891 and 1893, after plans drawn up by the architecture firm Perrault, Mesnard et Venne. Its eclectic style reflects the nationalist aspirations of its founders. The Monument-National was one of the first popular universities in Canada, the largest Yiddish cultural centre in North America and the birthplace of Quebec's first feminist and associative movements. Between 1893 and 1993 over 1,000 politicians and intellectuals gave speeches in this building, and nearly 10,000 shows, concerts and original productions by Quebec artists graced its stages. Restored in 1993, the Monument-National has housed the National Theatre School of Canada since 1971.

Year designated: 1985
Location: plaque erected at 1182 Saint-Laurent Boulevard.

Marie Lacoste-Gérin-Lajoie (1867-1945)

A pioneer in the defence of women's rights in Canada, Marie Lacoste-Gérin-Lajoie co-founded and served as president of French Canada's most important feminist association, the Fédération nationale Saint-Jean-Baptiste (FNSJB), created in Montréal in 1907. In 1913 she launched the federation's magazine, *La Bonne Parole*, in which she championed a number of causes, mainly women's suffrage and their access to higher education, as well as improvements in their legal status. Her efforts in the latter sphere led to the reform of Quebec's Civil Code in 1931. The secretariat of the Fédération nationale Saint-Jean-Baptiste had its offices in the Monument-National until 1925.

Year designated: 1997
Proposed location: Monument-National, 1182 Saint-Laurent Boulevard; plaque to be erected.

66 The Monument-National in 1894.
BNQ, Albums E.-Z. Massicotte, Albums de rues, 7-34-a.
67 Marie Lacoste-Gérin-Lajoie.
Archives de l'Institut Notre-Dame du Bon-Conseil de Montréal.

Idola Saint-Jean
(1880-1945)

Idola Saint-Jean taught French and diction in various schools in Montréal as well as at the Monument-National, where she gave evening courses. In addition to pursuing a career in teaching, she played a leading role in the fight for women's equality, social justice, human rights and world peace. Between 1920 and 1940 she campaigned for the recognition of women's right to vote in Quebec. A woman of letters and a talented speaker, she never hesitated to use these qualities to serve the causes she defended.

DOWNTOWN

Year designated: 1997
Location: plaque erected at 1182 Saint-Laurent Boulevard.

(68) Idola Saint-Jean, ca. 1940-1945, Studio Garcia.
NAC, C-068508.

Wilfrid Pelletier
(1896-1982)

This internationally renowned conductor is one of the most important figures in the history of Quebec music. He made an outstanding contribution to the development of opera in the province and as of 1936 devoted considerable effort to organizing major concert series, such as the Montreal Festivals and the Matinées symphoniques pour la jeunesse. In 1942 he founded the Conservatoire de musique et d'art dramatique du Québec, which he directed until 1961. Between 1951 and 1966 Wilfrid Pelletier was the artistic director of the Québec and Montréal symphony orchestras and the province's music teaching program. He won numerous honours in the course of his career, including Companion of the Order of Canada in 1967. One of the performance halls in Montréal's Place des Arts is named after him.

Year designated: 1988
Location: plaque erected in Place des Arts, Salle Wilfrid-Pelletier,
260 De Maisonneuve Boulevard West.

William Notman
(1826-1891)

Notman was not only the most famous Canadian photographer of the 19th century, but a portrait photographer of international repute. This talented man, who moved to Montréal in 1856, has left us countless portraits of the leading figures of his day as well as thousands of photographs of his city of adoption, Canada and the eastern United States. By the 1880s he had built up a photographic firm with over 20 branch studios, including seven in Canada. His studio in Montréal was a veritable arts centre, where painting and sculpture exhibitions were often held. Notman's photographic archives, which have been assembled at the McCord Museum of Canadian History since 1956, are an invaluable source of iconography.

Year designated: 1975
Proposed location: former Notman residence, 51 Sherbrooke Street West;
plaque to be erected.

(69) Wilfrid Pelletier.
Montreal Symphony Orchestra Archives.
(70) William Notman, photographer, 1866-1867.
McCord Museum of Canadian History, Montréal, I-24151.1.

Émile Nelligan (1879-1941)

Émile Nelligan, who is probably French Canada's most beloved and admired poet, wrote some 170 poems, sonnets, rondeaux and songs during his short literary career. Suffering from mental problems, he was committed to the Saint-Benoît Asylum in 1899 and then transferred to Saint-Jean-de-Dieu Psychiatric Hospital, where he lived until his death on November 18, 1941. His poem *Romance du vin* and his unforgettable *Vaisseau d'or* contributed greatly to his renown. Nelligan's poetic vision has endured thanks to the publication of his complete works and to the numerous conferences, films, novels, and even a ballet and an opera produced in his honour. Since 1979, the Prix Émile-Nelligan has been awarded annually to a talented young Canadian poet.

Year designated: 1974
Proposed location: Saint-Louis Square, northwest of Sherbrooke Street, next to Saint-Denis; plaque to be erected.

71 Émile Nelligan in 1904.
NAC, C-088566.

Pavillon Mailloux

72

Like several other nurses' residences erected in Canada in the early 20th century, this building, constructed in 1932, bears witness to the national historic significance of the nursing profession in this country. At the time, such residences were specially designed to meet the training needs of future nurses, while providing these young women with a place where they could relax in a family-like setting. The quality of the teaching provided here has contributed significantly over the years to winning recognition for the professional status of nurses. Pavillon Mailloux, which is now part of the vast Notre-Dame Hospital complex, has undergone numerous renovations, and only one of its lounges is still in its original state.

Year designated: 1997
Location: Notre-Dame Hospital, 1560 Sherbrooke Street East; plaque to be erected.

The *Accommodation*

73

Built and launched in Montréal in 1809, the *Accommodation* was the first steamship to be put into service in Canada. Owned by the brewer John Molson, this "steam-powered rowboat," as *The Gazette* called it at the time, took 36 hours to travel from Montréal to Québec City on its maiden voyage. Its engines, which were built at the Forges du Saint-Maurice, drove two side-mounted paddle wheels. The ship could also be powered by sail if its engines failed. Even though the *Accommodation* was a commercial failure, it was the forerunner of the dozens of steamships that later plied Canada's waters. The vessel was scrapped in 1811.

Year designated: 1925
Location: plaque erected in Molson Park, opposite 1670 Notre-Dame Street East, at the corner of Papineau.

72 Pavillon Mailloux.
    Photo: Rémi Chénier, Parks Canada, Québec, November 2003.
73 Launching of the *Accommodation* in 1809, A. Sherriff Scott.
    NAC, C-148638, original in the Molson Archives.

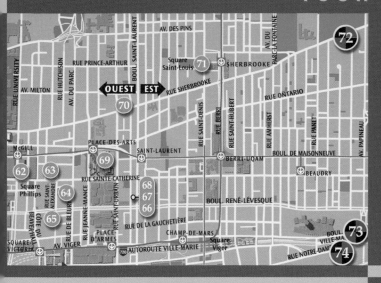

William Molson
(1793-1875)

A member of the famous Molson family of Montréal, William was one of the leading entrepreneurs of his day. A brewer, distiller, merchant and banker, he excelled in several key sectors of the Canadian economy, including the beer and liquor industry, steam navigation, the import and retail trades, railways, mining and natural gas. In 1853 he founded the Molsons Bank, which merged with the Bank of Montreal in 1925. The former head office of the Molsons Bank can still be seen on the southeast corner of Saint-Pierre and Saint-Jacques streets.

Year designated: 1971
Proposed location: Molson's Brewery, 1500 Notre-Dame Street East; plaque to be erected.

DOWNTOWN

THE ISLAND O

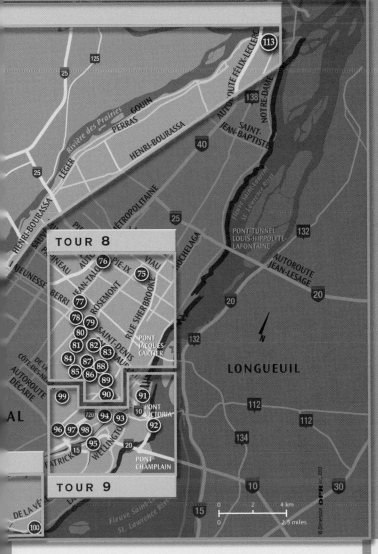

THE ISLAND OF MONTRÉAL

Brother Marie-Victorin (1885-1944)

Conrad Kirouac (Brother Marie-Victorin) was born on April 3, 1885, in Kingsey Falls, in the Eastern Townships. He learned the basics of botany at the novitiate of the Brothers of the Christian Schools in Montréal and at Longueuil College, with Brother Rolland-Germain. As of the late 1920s he was at the forefront of the scientific movement in Quebec, and even in Canada as a whole. Brother Marie-Victorin lives on through his accomplishments as an ecclesiastic, a scientist and a teacher. One of his most important legacies, apart from his book *Flore laurentienne* and Montréal's Botanical Garden, is the multitude of scholars and thinkers he trained with a view to inspiring them toward the following ideal: "Instill in our hearts the firm conviction that knowledge, science, nature, love and faith are but one and the same thing. Brandish with humility, but also courage, in a single hand, the two divine torches of knowledge and love, and strive to pass them to other men."

Year designated: 1987
Location: plaque erected at the main entrance to the Botanical Garden, 4101 Sherbrooke Street East, at the corner of Pie-IX Boulevard.

(75) Brother Marie-Victorin at his desk.
Photo: Montréal Botanical Garden.

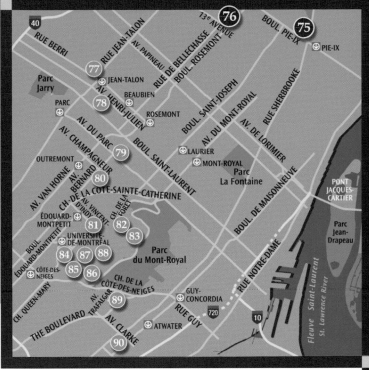

George Beers
(1841-1900)

This eminent Montréal dentist established the rules for lacrosse and popularized this game of Amerindian origin in the second half of the 19th century. A lacrosse enthusiast, he wanted to make the sport less violent and standardize the way it was played. The rules he published in 1860 were adopted by the National Lacrosse Association in 1867, and around the end of the 19th century the game was raised to the rank of a national sport largely as a result of Beers' efforts. Interest for lacrosse grew continually among Canadians up to the First World War.

Year designated: 1976
Proposed location: Étienne-Desmarteaux Centre, 3430 de Bellechasse Street, at the corner of 13e Avenue; plaque to be erected.

(76) Messrs. Beers (right) and Stevenson playing lacrosse in 1868, William Notman. McCord Museum of Canadian History, Montréal, I-35122.1.

THE ISLAND OF MONTRÉAL

77

St. George Antiochian Orthodox Church

This church was built by Raoul Gariépy in 1939-1940 to serve the oldest and largest Syrian-Lebanese Orthodox community in Canada. The building displays a combination of Byzantine and Western features. The Byzantine influence can be seen in the central dome, the domes of the two bell-towers, the arched windows and the interior layout, which includes a narthex, or vestibule, a nave and a sanctuary. The sanctuary is separated from the nave by an iconostasis, or an openwork partition embellished with icons. In keeping with the precepts of Byzantine architecture, the transept is not very large and the ceiling is vaulted. A Western influence is reflected in the twin bell-towers, the pediment on the façade, the central door flanked by two other entrances, the large stairway leading to the street and the contrast between the yellow brick and the paler-toned limestone. All of the windows are stained-glass. These features, which are uncommon in an Orthodox church, testify to the integration of the Syrian-Lebanese community into Western society. The interior decoration of this religious monument is the work of artist Emmanuel Briffa. The church is still used to celebrate religious holidays and rites that continue to hold meaning for the descendants of the first Syrians to arrive in Canada in the late 19th century.

Year designated: 1999
Location: plaque erected at 555-575 Jean-Talon Street East, on the corner of Lajeunesse.

77 St. George Antiochian Orthodox Church.
Photo: Rémi Chénier, Parks Canada, Québec, November 2003.

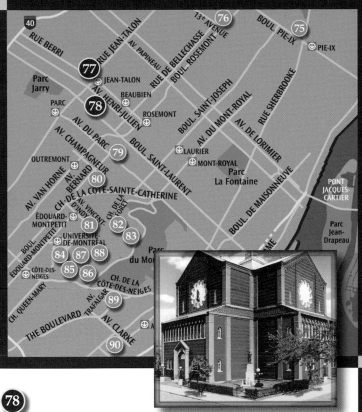

77
78

Church of Notre-Dame-de-la-Défense

Large-scale Italian immigration to Canada began in the 1890s and many Italian immigrants settled in Montréal. In 1910 the Archbishop of Montréal, Mgr. Bruchési created Notre-Dame-de-la-Défense as a national parish in the heart of Little Italy to serve the members of this community in their own language. In 1918-1919 the parish council had a church built to the plans of Guido Nincheri, an Italian artist who had recently arrived in Canada; Nincheri worked on the project with the Montréal architecture firm Roch Montbriant. The style of architecture chosen for the building is a local expression of the Italian Romanesque Revival. Guido Nincheri also designed the church's interior decor and painted the magnificent frescoes and murals. The decoration work began in 1924, continued from 1927 to 1933 and was completed only in the 1960s. The presbytery was added in 1955 and the chapel around 1962-1964. The Chiesa della Madonna della Difesa, which is considered the earliest surviving church built specially for the Italian-Canadian community in Montréal, the oldest such community in Canada, is also considered by Italian Canadians as their mother church. Italian Canadians from all walks of life come here in large numbers to celebrate baptisms, marriages, funerals and annual holidays.

Year designated: 2002
Location: 6800 Henri-Julien Avenue, at the corner of Dante Street; plaque to be erected.

78 Church of Notre-Dame-de-la-Défense, retouched view.

THE ISLAND OF MONTRÉAL

Rialto Theatre

This theatre designed by Emmanuel Briffa, with its façade inspired by the Paris Opera and perfectly harmonized with its Baroque interior decor, is an outstanding example of movie theatre architecture in Canada. Built in 1923-1924 after the plans of architect Joseph-Raoul Gariépy, it bears eloquent testimony to the era when luxury movie theatres were erected in new city districts, not only in Montréal but elsewhere in Canada. Up to the time it closed in 1992, the Rialto served as a movie theatre, except on a few occasions beginning in 1988, when it was used as a venue for other forms of entertainment. The building was declared an historic monument by the Ministère de la Culture et des Communications du Québec in 1990.

Year designated: 1993
Location: 5711 du Parc Avenue;
plaque to be erected.

Outremont Theatre

This building, which was inaugurated in 1929, is typical of the luxurious movie theatres built at that time in new city districts and suburbs. Its most distinctive feature is the combining of two stylistic influences that marked movie theatre design in the 1920s. Its exterior is characteristic of the Early Art Deco period, while its rich interior combines features of the "atmospheric" and Art Deco styles. The building's exceptional state of preservation adds to its historical and architectural interest. Ten years after it was closed in 1991, the Outremont Theatre was reopened as a variety show venue.

Year designated: 1993
Location: 1240-1248 Bernard Avenue West, at the corner of Champagneur;
plaque to be erected.

(79) Rialto Theatre, 1936.
Ville de Montréal. Gestion de documents et archives. VM94- Z119.
(80) Outremont Theatre, ca. 1940, Hayward Studios.
NAC, PA-81560.

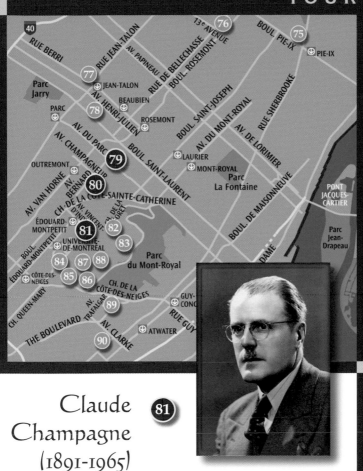

Claude Champagne (1891-1965)

(81)

Due to his admiration for Claude Debussy, Joseph-Arthur-Adonaï Champagne changed his first name to Claude around 1917. In 1927 he decided to devote himself to teaching since there were very few employment opportunities in composing. Champagne enjoyed a very diversified career as a teacher, in addition to taking on a host of administrative duties. The year 1964 was declared "Claude-Champagne Year" in honour of this man who was a pioneer not only as a composer and musician, but also as a teacher and administrator. According to Claude Champagne, his source of inspiration was quite simple: "I was always much impressed with nature. Other interviewers have asked me what was the strongest influence in my life, and I told them nature, as far as my work was concerned." *Suite canadienne* (1927), *Symphonie gaspésienne* (1947) and *Altitude* (1959) are some of his most important works.

Year designated: 1988
Location: plaque erected at the music faculty of Université de Montréal, 200 Vincent-d'Indy Avenue.

(81) Claude Champagne, before 1948.
National Library of Canada, negative number NL 15349.

THE ISLAND OF MONTRÉAL

Mount Royal Cemetery

This Protestant cemetery, which was laid out on the north slope of Mount Royal as of 1852, is in keeping with the tradition of American rural cemeteries. In this cemetery, considerable importance is attached to the natural setting, which is conducive to strolling and meditation. The tombstones are skillfully integrated with the imaginatively landscaped grounds, creating a peaceful atmosphere for visitors. On account of its size, excellent design and the artistic and historical interest of its gravestones, this cemetery is one of the most beautiful garden cemeteries in North America. It is also a delightful spot to take walks, go bird watching and observe trees.

Year designated: 1998
Proposed location: entrance to Mount Royal Cemetery, 1297 de la Forêt Road; plaque to be erected.

Sir Alexander Tilloch Galt (1817-1893)

Alexander Tilloch Galt was one of the Fathers of the Canadian Confederation of 1867. Of Scottish descent, he moved to Canada in 1835 and became active in land speculation, business, and railway construction. Through a combination of circumstances, Galt made his debut in politics in 1849 as a member of the Legislative Assembly for the riding of Sherbrooke. He cherished a vision of a federation of the British colonies in North America, which prompted him to draft his first plan for confederation in 1858. He took part in the Charlottetown and Québec conferences of 1864 as well as in the one in London in 1866. His key role in the process that gave birth to the new Canadian state was underscored by the audience Queen Victoria granted him on February 27, 1867.

Year designated: 1967
Location: Fathers of Confederation plaque erected on a monument in Mount Royal Cemetery, plot F-11, 1297 de la Forêt Road.

82 Entrance to Mount Royal Cemetery.
BNQ, Albums E.-Z. Massicotte, Albums de rues, 3-39-c.
83 Sir Alexander T. Galt in 1869, William James Topley.
NAC, PA-013008.

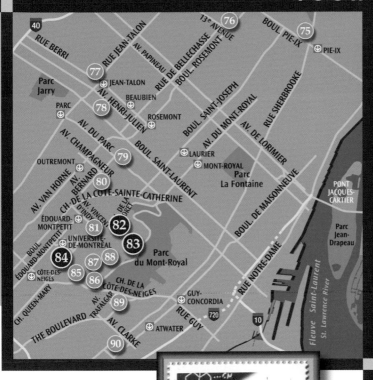

Hans Selye
(1907-1982)

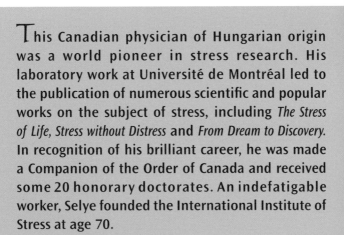

Canada 46

This Canadian physician of Hungarian origin was a world pioneer in stress research. His laboratory work at Université de Montréal led to the publication of numerous scientific and popular works on the subject of stress, including *The Stress of Life*, *Stress without Distress* and *From Dream to Discovery*. In recognition of his brilliant career, he was made a Companion of the Order of Canada and received some 20 honorary doctorates. An indefatigable worker, Selye founded the International Institute of Stress at age 70.

Year designated: 1989
Proposed location: medical faculty, Université de Montréal, 2900 de la Tour Road; plaque to be erected.

84 Dr. Hans Selye, commemorative stamp issued in 2000.
"© Canada Post Corporation, 2000. Reproduced with permission."

THE ISLAND OF MONTRÉAL

Notre-Dame-des-Neiges Cemetery

Notre-Dame-des-Neiges Cemetery on majestic Mount Royal was inaugurated in 1855. The fact that it was placed beyond the city limits reflects the "rural cemetery" trend that emerged in North America in 1831. This Catholic cemetery is one of the most remarkable of its day because of its size, beautiful layout and the architectural, artistic and historic value of its tombstones. A number of famous Canadians are buried here, including Sir George-Étienne Cartier, Émile Nelligan and Mary Travers (La Bolduc).

Year designated: 1998
Proposed location: entrance to Notre-Dame-des-Neiges Cemetery,
4601 Côte-des-Neiges Road;
plaque to be erected.

Sir George-Étienne Cartier (1814-1873) 86

Lawyer, railway promoter and, above all, brilliant politician, Cartier won considerable renown in Canadian politics in the mid 19th century. Co-Prime Minister of the Province of Canada from 1857 to 1862, he championed many bills favourable to his French-Canadian compatriots in the legal, judicial and education sectors. However, his crowning political achievement was the role he played in bringing about the birth of the Canadian Confederation. Cartier was also one of the main architects of the country's westward expansion around 1870.

Year designated: 1959
Location: plaque erected on the back of the monument to G.-É. Cartier in Notre-Dame-des-Neiges Cemetery, plot O-1, 4601 Côte-des-Neiges Road.

85 Entrance to Notre-Dame-des-Neiges Cemetery, ca. 1897.
BNQ, Albums E.-Z. Massicotte, Albums de rues, I-135-c.
86 Sir George-Étienne Cartier, ca. 1871, drawn after a photograph by William Notman & Son.
NAC, C-002728.

87
Thomas D'Arcy McGee
(1825-1868)

Journalist, poet, historian and politician, Thomas D'Arcy McGee is considered one of the most eloquent of the Fathers of Confederation. He settled in Montréal in 1857 at the request of the city's Irish community. There he founded the newspaper *New Era*, in which he defended the rights of the Irish and explained his vision of a British North American federation. The Reform Party member for Montréal in 1858, he switched to the Conservative Party in 1863, finding its policies to be more in keeping with his plans for national development. Appointed Minister of Agriculture, Immigration and Statistics, he was one of the Canadian delegates to the Charlottetown and Québec conferences of 1864 leading to the birth of Confederation. In addition to his many speeches and newspaper articles, McGee wrote several books on the history of Ireland as well as more than 300 poems. He was assassinated in Ottawa on April 7, 1868, possibly as a result of a conspiracy by Irish patriots belonging to the American Fenian movement.

Year designated: 1959
Location: plaque erected on a mausoleum in Notre-Dame-des-Neiges cemetery, plot K12-32, 4601 Côte-des-Neiges Road.

(87) Thomas D'Arcy McGee in 1867, William Notman.
NAC, C-016749.

Michel Bibaud
(1782-1857)

Born on Côte-des-Neiges Road, Bibaud was a teacher, journalist, author and annalist. An occasional poet, he published the first collection of poetry by a French Canadian to appear in Canada: *Épîtres, satires, chansons, épigrammes et autres pièces de vers*. As a journalist, he wrote articles for several historical, scientific and literary periodicals, particularly *Bibliothèque canadienne*, a monthly journal he founded in 1825. His two-volume work *Histoire du Canada* elicited a range of reactions because of its decidedly Loyalist flavour.

Year designated: 1945
Location: plaque erected near the entrance to Notre-Dame-des-Neiges Cemetery, opposite 4505 Côte-des-Neiges Road.

Trafalgar Lodge

Trafalgar Lodge is one of the few examples of Gothic Revival residential architecture found in Quebec, the style being confined mainly to the Atlantic Provinces and Ontario. Designed by John Howard, this large house was built between 1846 and 1848 for Albert Furniss, Senior Manager of the Montreal Gas Company and a highly influential figure in political and economic circles. Despite the many changes the building has undergone since its construction, several of its features still reflect the "rationalist, archaeological" phase that emerged in the Gothic Revival style around 1850: for example, the rose window in the front door, the cut-out clover motifs and the gingerbread fascia boards.

Year designated: 1990
Proposed location: 3021 Trafalgar Avenue;
plaque to be erected.

Church of Saint-Léon de Westmount

The interior decoration of this beautiful church was done in 1928 and 1944 by Guido Nincheri, a Canadian artist of Italian origin who worked on the ornamentation of over 50 buildings in Canada. The Church of Saint-Léon de Westmount is one of the most representative examples of Nincheri's work, in that it illustrates his manifold talents as an architect, sculptor, painter, stained-glass artist and designer. In the 1930s Nincheri was honoured on four separate occasions by the Vatican, which hailed him as one the greatest religious artists in the world.

Year designated: 1997
Location: plaque erected at
4311 De Maisonneuve Boulevard West.

THE ISLAND OF MONTRÉAL

⑨⓪ Church of Saint-Léon de Westmount.
Photo: Rémi Chénier, Parks Canada, Québec, November 2003.

The Lachine Canal (91)

The Lachine Canal was dug between 1821 and 1825 in the wake of canal-building work in Great Britain at the end of the 18th century. Widened in the 1840s and 1870s, it was the head of a canal system on the St. Lawrence River linking the Atlantic Ocean with the Great Lakes and forming the longest inland navigation corridor in the world. Designed primarily for ships, the Lachine Canal differed from British canals of the period, which were used mainly by barges. Part of the canal was closed to navigation in 1960, and 10 years later the entire structure was shut down. Over the years, through the efforts of skilled engineers, the canal had come to play a triple role, serving as a navigable waterway, a power source and an industrial water supply. However, the last two roles conflicted with its main one, and major upgrading work was needed, especially in the 19th century, to reconcile the canal's different functions. Although sailing vessels and then steamships used the Lachine Canal, a new type of boat eventually had to be designed for it. Known as a canaller, the boat was specially adapted to the size of the canal's locks as well as to that of the locks of all the other canals on the inland navigation system. Three main products were ferried through the Lachine Canal in the course of its history: first, wood from land cleared for colonization in Ontario, and then wheat and flour. Coal from Pennsylvania and Nova Scotia was shipped through it as well in later years. The Lachine Canal was reopened to navigation in May 2002.

Year designated: 1929
Proposed location: a plaque at each end of the canal,
i.e. near the Old Port and in Lachine; plaques to be erected.

(91) Lachine Canal, ca. 1850, James Duncan.
McCord Museum of Canadian History, Montréal, M984.273.

Construction of the Victoria Tubular Bridge

Built between 1854 and 1859, the Victoria Tubular Bridge was the most ambitious project of its kind ever undertaken up to that time anywhere in the world. Owing to its special design, its innovative construction and the type of materials used, it marked the beginning of a new era in railway bridge construction. When it was brought into service in 1860, it had a major impact on the economic development of Montréal and Canada as a whole. It was demolished in 1897 and replaced by a steel lattice-girder structure with two railway tracks. Known as the Victoria Jubilee Bridge, the new structure rested on the abutments and piers of the original bridge.

Year designated: 1999
Proposed location: south entrance to the Victoria Bridge or beside the bicycle path in Saint-Lambert; plaque to be erected.

92 Victoria Bridge (*De Victoria Brug Te Montreal*), 19th-century etching printed by E. Spanier, The Hague. BNQ, Montréal, iconodoc. 092.

Lachine Canal Manufacturing Complex

The Lachine Canal, which marks the transition between deep-sea shipping and inland navigation, is considered the birthplace of Canada's manufacturing industry. It formed a huge hydraulic power complex that gave rise to one of the largest manufacturing centres in the country. Several factors contributed to this phenomenon. First of all, the water in the canal provided the motive

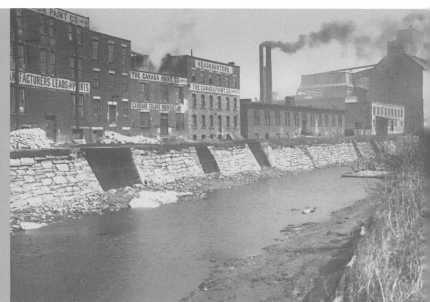

93a

Year designated: 1996
Proposed location: near the Saint-Gabriel Lock,
at the corner of Des Seigneurs and Basin streets; plaque to be erected.

93   Lachine Canal, ca. 1930. ANQQ, E21 ministère des Terres et Forêts / Série compagnie aérienne franco-canadienne no. N49-16.

93a   Lachine Canal above the Saint-Gabriel Lock, 1920. NAC, PA-10118.

93b

power needed to operate factories, in addition to supplying a bleaching, cleaning and cooling agent. Secondly, the transportation possibilities offered by the canal in combination with Montréal's railway hub attracted industry to the area. And thirdly, the ensuing concentration of an exceptionally wide range of businesses helped to create a network of interdependency, which proved crucial to the success of this industrial complex. Other important factors were the presence of a labour pool and the proximity of a large urban, business and financial centre. Between 1846 and 1945 close to 800 businesses from all production sectors, including many of the technological flagships of Canadian industry, built facilities along the canal.

THE ISLAND OF MONTRÉAL

93b Basin No. 2 of the Lachine Canal. Livingston Linseed Oil Co. in 1903.
Parks Canada Collection, Quebec Service Centre.

Bank of Montreal Building

The Des Seigneurs Street branch of the Bank of Montreal was built between 1894 and 1895 according to the plans of architect Sir Andrew Thomas Taylor. The main characteristics of this Queen Anne Revival building are its red sandstone facing and large, elaborate dormer windows, as well as its bays framed by pilasters supporting carved winged cerberuses or lions bearing shields. The branch opened on May 1, 1895, and closed on August 31, 1979.

Year designated: 1990
Location: 1850 Notre-Dame Street West, at the corner of Des Seigneurs; plaque to be erected.

Merchants Manufacturing Company

The Merchants Manufacturing Company, founded in 1880, set up operations in the Montréal suburb of Saint-Henri by erecting a textile mill there in 1881. The mill building, which was made of brick, measured 115 metres long by 25 metres wide and had 4 storeys, not including the basement. Up and running as of 1882, the plant was enlarged in the 1890s. Between 1885 and 1908 additional equipment was installed, bringing the number of spindles from 25,500 to 110,000 and the number of looms from 635 to 2,465. The textile mill thus became the second largest of its kind in Canada. The facility produced white shirting, unbleached and deluxe cotton cloth, sheets, pillowcases, gauze and other types of dyed or bleached cotton fabric. Merchants was an independent company until 1905, when it merged with Dominion Textile. The mill closed in 1967. This building, which has now been converted into condominiums, is one of the last testaments to the Lachine Canal's role as the birthplace of Canadian industry.

Year designated: 1989
Proposed location: 3970-4200 Saint-Ambroise Street, at the corner of Saint-Ferdinand; plaque to be erected.

(94) Bank of Montreal, ca. 1895, William Notman & Son.
McCord Museum of Canadian History, Montréal, VIEW-2794.
(95) Merchants Manufacturing Company, ca. 1893.
Published in *A Chronology of Montreal and of Canada from A.D. 1752 to A.D. 1893*, p. 355.

Marguerite Bourgeoys
(1620-1700)

A number of women, because of their courage and dedication, will live forever in the collective memory of Canadians. Marguerite Bourgeoys is one of them. From the time she arrived in New France in 1653, she devoted herself to providing free education to girls in the fledgling colony. Today, her work is pursued throughout Canada, the United States and Japan by the nuns of Canada's first religious community, the Congrégation de Notre-Dame, which Marguerite Bourgeoys founded in 1658. Canonized by the Vatican in 1982, Marguerite Bourgeoys was the first Canadian woman to receive this honour.

THE ISLAND OF MONTRÉAL

Year designated: 1985
Location: plaque erected on the grounds of Villa Maria High School, 4245 Décarie Boulevard, at the corner of Monkland.

96 Authentic portrait of Marguerite Bourgeoys, 1700, Pierre Le Ber.
Marguerite-Bourgeoys Museum, 1999.128. Photo: Bernard Dubois.

James Bruce, 8th Earl of Elgin (1811-1863)

From 1847 to 1849, as governor general of Canada, James Bruce lived in the house called Monklands, which is now occupied by Villa Maria High School. This diplomat gained renown in Canada's political arena on numerous occasions. He caused quite a stir in 1849, when he introduced a bill to compensate victims for losses suffered during the Uprisings of 1837 and 1838. The ensuing outcry culminated in the torching of Montréal's Parliament Buildings and in fights in the city's streets. Lord Elgin left Canadian politics in 1854 and retired to England. He died in 1863 while serving as viceroy and governor general of India.

Year designated: 1974
Proposed location: Villa Maria High School, 4245 Décarie Boulevard, at the corner of Monkland; plaque to be erected.

Villa Maria Convent

This magnificent residence was originally known as Monklands, after James Monk, Chief Justice of the Court of King's Bench, who erected the main part of the building in 1794. From 1844 to 1849, this house served as the principal residence for three of Canada's governors general: Sir Charles Metcalfe, Lord Cathcart and Lord Elgin. In April 1854, the property was sold to the Congrégation de Notre-Dame of Montréal and then converted into a convent for young girls and renamed Villa Maria. The nuns of the Congrégation de Notre-Dame still own the building and continue to teach here.

Year designated: 1951
Proposed location: 4245 Décarie Boulevard, at the corner of Monkland; plaque to be erected.

97 *James Bruce, The Earl of Elgin and Kincardine,* 1848, Thomas Coffin Doane. NAC, C-000291.
98 *Monklands, Villa Maria Convent,* ca. 1889, William Notman & Son. McCord Museum of Canadian History, Montréal, VIEW-1919.

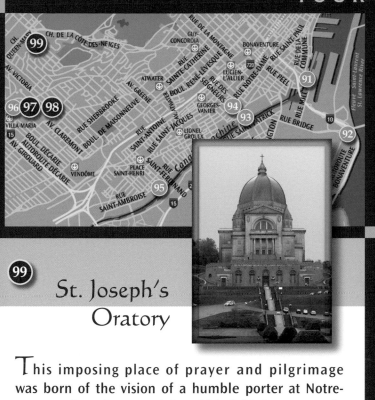

97
98
99

99 St. Joseph's Oratory

This imposing place of prayer and pilgrimage was born of the vision of a humble porter at Notre-Dame College in Montréal and his faith in St. Joseph. Alfred Bessette (better known as Brother André, of the Congregation of Holy Cross) initiated the construction of the first chapel dedicated to Canada's patron saint on Mount Royal in 1904. As the number of visitors to the site increased, the chapel had to be enlarged, first in 1908 and again in 1910. In 1917 a church, or crypt, with a seating capacity of 1,000 was erected. A few years later remarkable stained-glass windows by Perdriau and O'Shea Workshops were installed in the building. Construction work began on the basilica in 1924, following the plans of Dalbé Viau and Alphonse Venne. In 1937, the year Brother André died, Dom Paul Bellot, a French Benedictine monk, and Lucien Parent, a Montréal architect, started the exterior finishing work. The building's interior decoration, entrusted to Gérard Notebaert, continued to be worked on until 1966; among its most notable features are the magnificent stained-glass windows by Marius Plamondon and the statues of the 12 apostles by Henri Charlier. The oratory complex also includes a votive chapel, a museum, a garden and a Way of the Cross on the mountain by sculptor Louis Parent. Brother André was beatified by Pope John Paul II in 1982. He never would have imagined that the oratory would welcome over 2,000,000 people a year as it does now.

Year designated: 2003
Proposed location: 3800 Queen Mary Road; plaque to be erected.

99 St. Joseph's Oratory.
Photo: Jean-François Caron, Parks Canada, Québec, October 2003.

THE ISLAND OF MONTRÉAL

The Lachine Rapids

For water sports enthusiasts, these rapids are synonymous with fun and excitement. However, they long constituted an obstacle to shipping between eastern and western Canada, obliging people and goods to travel by land between Montréal and Lachine. As a result, the Montréal area became a major transit, trade and storage centre. The Lachine Rapids thus played a key role in the development of Montréal and the surrounding area. With the opening of the Lachine Canal in 1824, the St. Lawrence River was linked with the Great Lakes, making it much easier to reach the interior.

Year designated: 1982
Location: plaque erected on LaSalle Boulevard in LaSalle, between Champlain and Bishop Power boulevards.

Le Ber-Le Moyne House

This house, located on the grounds of the Lachine Museum, was built between 1669 and 1671 as a trading post for two eminent Montréal merchants, Jacques Le Ber and Charles Le Moyne. The westernmost post in the colony, it remained in operation until 1685. The house was later sold and then ravaged by fire in 1689, probably during the "Lachine massacre;" it remained abandoned until 1695. Repair work was eventually undertaken, and the building served as a private residence until 1946, when it was purchased by the municipality of Lachine. A museum was opened within its walls in 1948 and extensive renovations were carried out between 1980 and 1985. Based on available information, the Le Ber-Le Moyne House and one of its outbuildings known as the *dépendance* are the only "still-standing" remains of a French-Regime trading post in Canada.

Year designated: 2002
Location: 110 de LaSalle Road, Lachine; plaque to be erected.

(100) Boat descending the Lachine Rapids, 1843, H. F. Ainslie. NAC, C-000506.

(101) Le Ber-Le Moyne House, ca. 1671, in Désiré Girouard, *Le vieux Lachine et le massacre du 5 août 1689* (Montréal: Gebhardt-Berthiaume), 1889.

The Lachine Stone Warehouse

THE ISLAND OF MONTRÉAL

This building, which was much smaller when it was built in 1803, is interesting because of its close links to the fur trade in the first half of the 19th century. Its original owners, Alexander Gordon and the Hudson's Bay Company, used it for storing fur trade goods until 1859. The building was eventually sold to the Sisters of Saint Anne and modified extensively to convert it into housing. Parks Canada has owned the building since 1977 and uses it to commemorate the fur trade, one of the most important chapters in Canadian history.

Year designated: 1970
Location: plaque erected in Monk Park at The Fur Trade at Lachine National Historic Site of Canada, to the left of the warehouse's façade, near Saint-Joseph Boulevard and 12e Avenue, Lachine.

Lachine Massacre

The Lachine massacre marked the climax of the war between the French and the Iroquois for control of trading territories in the 17th century. In June 1687 the Marquis de Denonville, Governor of New France, treacherously imprisoned over 100 Iroquois, many of whom were later sent to France to serve in the King's galleys. To avenge this affront, a band of 1,500 Iroquois invaded Lachine on the night of August 4-5, 1689, and massacred the inhabitants. Based on reports from the period, 2,000 people were killed and 120 others were taken prisoner. It seems more likely, however, that a total of 100 or so people died. Whatever the case may be, this tragic event terrorized the entire colony. For many years, the year 1689 was known as the "year of the massacre." Hostilities ended with the signing of the Treaty of Montréal in August 1701.

Year designated: 1923
Location: plaque erected at the entrance to The Fur Trade at Lachine National Historic Site of Canada, 1255 Saint-Joseph Boulevard, Lachine.

Sisters of Saint Anne

The Sisters of Saint Anne are one of the religious communities that have contributed the most to the development of Canadian society. Ever since the community was founded by Marie-Esther Blondin in 1850, it has continued to grow and diversify its activities, particularly by providing instruction to children and adults in several Canadian provinces and in the United States. The nuns have also devoted themselves to caring for the sick and the elderly in hospitals and to operating shelters and clinics. In addition, they have taken part in various movements for social justice, youth assistance and the advancement of women, as well as offering volunteer and pastoral services.

Year designated: 1988
Location: plaque erected near the main entrance to the Sainte-Anne Convent, 1300 Saint-Joseph Boulevard, Lachine.

(103) *Fugitive, épisode du massacre de Lachine, 1689*, bronze sculpture by Louis-Philippe Hébert, 1910. Musée national des beaux-arts du Québec, accession number 73.12. Photo: Patrick Altman.

(104) **The venerable Marie-Esther Blondin, founder of the Sisters of Saint Anne, after 1850.** Archives of the Sisters of Saint Anne.

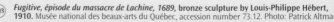
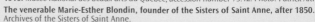

Cavelier de La Salle
(1643-1687)

René-Robert Cavelier de La Salle, a native of Rouen, France, was one of Canada's greatest explorers. When he arrived in this country in 1667, he founded a small village, which he named "Coste St Sulpice," in the western part of the Island of Montréal in the area now known as Lachine. A true adventurer, La Salle abandoned the sedentary life and set out in 1669 to explore the Mississippi River. Through his expeditions, he became one of the first to navigate the Great Lakes. In 1675 he was granted Fort Cataracoui, which he renamed Fort Frontenac. La Salle reached the mouth of the Mississippi on April 6, 1682, and on April 9 he officially took possession of the area in the name of France. He thus allowed France to extend its territory to the Gulf of Mexico.

Year designated: 1934
Location: plaque erected on a monument on Promenade du Père-Marquette, between 17e Avenue and 18e Avenue, Lachine.

(105) René-Robert Cavelier de La Salle, lithograph by Jules Adeline, ca. 1870.
ANQQ, E6, S8, P18259-Y-12.

THE ISLAND OF MONTRÉAL

Sir William Christopher Macdonald (1831-1917)

106

William Christopher, the founder of the famous Macdonald Tobacco Company, was born on Prince Edward Island. He moved to Montréal in 1852 and as of 1871 owned a tobacco factory on Water Street (De la Commune) that employed over 500 people. Four years later, in east-end Montréal, he built a new factory that employed more than 1,000 people and was the largest of its kind in Canada. Over the years, Macdonald amassed an enormous fortune and became known for his philanthropy, a distinction that earned him a knighthood in 1898. He may be considered the "father" of McGill University, to which he donated more than $13 million. A principal shareholder of the Bank of Montreal and the Royal Trust Company and a member of several boards of directors, including that of the Montreal General Hospital, he took a keen interest in education in rural areas, as shown by the college he founded and endowed in Sainte-Anne-de-Bellevue. Inaugurated in 1907, this institution, known as MacDonald College, originally offered educational programs in agriculture, home economics and teaching.

Year designated: 1974
Proposed location: MacDonald College, 21111 Lakeshore Road, Sainte-Anne-de-Bellevue; plaque to be erected.

Sainte-Anne-de-Bellevue Canal

107

Built for commercial purposes between 1840 and 1843, the Sainte-Anne-de-Bellevue Canal is part of Canada's national canal system. Situated at the confluence of the St. Lawrence and Ottawa rivers, it helped to link Montréal with Ottawa as well as Kingston, on the shores of Lake Ontario. The canal was modified substantially during widening and modernization work, and it has retained only a few of its original features. Since 1963 the canal has been open solely to pleasure craft. Parks Canada commemorates the commercial role it played in the 19th and 20th centuries.

Year designated: 1987
Location: 170 Sainte-Anne Street, Sainte-Anne-de-Bellevue; plaque to be erected.

(106) Sir William Christopher Macdonald in 1901, William Notman & Son.
McCord Museum of Canadian History, Montréal, II-137467.1.
(107) Sainte-Anne Lock.
Photo: Jacques Beardsell, Parks Canada, Québec, August 1991, 194/PA/PR7/SPD-00032.

"Voyageurs"

Voyageurs were hired men who transported fur trade goods for the North West Company (1779) and prominent Montréal merchants like Simon McTavish and James McGill, and every spring they left Lachine for the hinterland in brigades. Each brigade consisted of three *canots de maître*, or Montreal canoes, manned by a bowsman, a steersman and paddlers. Paddlers who had no experience were called *milieux*, or middlemen, as they were placed in the middle of the canoe. Each Montreal canoe had a carrying capacity of 4 tons, or 60 bundles of provisions and trade goods weighing 40 kilograms each. These men, whose courage, endurance and skill were legendary, made the incredibly difficult journey to the hinterland through a network of rivers, lakes and portages. The summer rendez-vous of their brigades brought together as many as 1,000 men at Grand Portage (Fort William) on the north shore of Lake Superior. There cargoes were exchanged as *the hivernants*, or winterers, who lived in the isolated trading posts, took in food supplies and trade goods, while the Montrealers loaded up their canoes with furs for the return voyage to Lachine, which took until early September. Voyageurs played a key role in exploring the St. Lawrence River, its tributaries and Canada's northwest.

Year designated: 1938
Proposed location: Sainte-Anne-de-Bellevue Canal,
170 Sainte-Anne Street, Sainte-Anne-de-Bellevue; plaque to be erected.

THE ISLAND OF MONTRÉAL

(108) Canoe manned by Voyageurs of the Hudson's Bay Company in 1869, by Frances Anne Hopkins.
NAC, C-002771.

Parc-nature de l'Anse-à-l'Orme
Parc agricole du Bois-de-la-Roche
Lac des Deux Montagnes
Arboretum Morgan
Limits of the Historic District
N

Senneville Historic District

The Senneville Historic District is situated at the western tip of the Island of Montréal. It comprises 82 homes situated on large wooded properties along Senneville Road, as well as numerous secondary buildings associated with these houses: employees' residences, tea houses, barns, stables and garages. It also encompasses the Anse-à-l'Orme Nature Park, the Bois-de-la-Roche Farm Park, the Morgan Arboretum and the Braeside Golf Club. This area was recognized as being of national historic significance in November 2001 because it illustrates the synergy that emerged at the turn of the 20th century between prominent Montréal businessmen and some of the leading architects and landscape designers in Canada at the time. The area also testifies to the development of the Picturesque movement and of vernacular and Arts and Crafts architecture from 1865 to 1930. A number of masterpieces of Canadian design and architecture are found here, including the Dow, Abbott, Todd, Angus, Meredith, Morgan and Forget residences and the Boisbriant estate, which belonged initially to J. J. C. Abbott, Prime Minister of Canada, and then to the Clouston family.

109a   Year designated: 2001
Proposed location: near the Boisbriant estate, on Senneville Road; plaque to be erected.

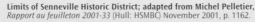

(109) Limits of Senneville Historic District; adapted from Michel Pelletier, *Rapport au feuilleton 2001-33* (Hull: HSMBC) November 2001, p. 1162.
(109a) J. L. Todd House, 180 Senneville Road.
Photo: Michel Pelletier, Parks Canada, Hull, 2001.

CH. SENNEVILLE 110

Parc-nature
du Bois-de-la-Roche

109

CH. SENNEVILLE

PONT DE
L'ÎLE-AUX-
TOURTES

CH. DES PINS

AUTOROUTE FÉLIX-LECLERC

Arboretum Morgan
Morgan Arboretum

CH. SAINTE-MARIE

BOUL. DES
ANCIENS-COMBATTANTS

40

CH. PACIFIC

AV.

CH. SENNEVILLE

107

BOUL
SAINTE

108

...IA DR.

110

LA BATAILLE DU
LAC DES DEUX MONTAGNES
THE BATTLE OF
THE LAKE OF TWO MOUNTAINS

Après le massacre de Lachine, en août 1689, des bandes
d'Iroquois continuèrent à semer la terreur dans le voisinage
de l'île de Montréal, sans provoquer de réaction de la part
des autorités de la colonie. Ce ne fut qu'au milieu
d'octobre que le gouverneur Denonville envoya Dulhut et
d'Ailleboust de Manthet en éclaireurs, accompagnés de 28
cadets. Au lac des Deux Montagnes, ils tombèrent sur un
parti de 22 Iroquois en canot. Ils en tuèrent 18, trois furent
fait prisonniers et un se sauva à la nage. Ce premier succès
redonna confiance aux habitants de la colonie.

Following the Lachine massacre in August 1689, the
Iroquois continued to terrorize the Montreal area. In October, Governor Denonville sent out a scouting party of 28
under the Sieurs Dulhut and d'Ailleboust de Manthet which
came upon a party of 22 Iroquois in the lac des Deux
Montagnes. In melee that followed this surprise en-
counter 18 Iroquois were killed, three taken prisoner, while
one swam to safety. This victory did much to restore the
shaken confidence of the inhabitants.

Commission des lieux et monuments historiques du Canada.
Historic Sites and Monuments Board of Canada.

Government du Canada · Government of Canada

110

The Battle of the Lake of Two Mountains

In the second half of the 17th century the French and the Iroquois were engaged in a struggle for control of trading territories. After the "Lachine massacre" of August 1689 bands of Iroquois continued to launch violent attacks on French colonists around the Island of Montréal. In October Governor Denonville sent out a patrol consisting of two soldiers by the name of Nicolas d'Ailleboust de Manthet and Greysolon Dulhut along with 28 cadets. When the contingent reached Lake of Two Mountains, they intercepted a group of 22 Iroquois in canoes. A battle broke out during which 18 Iroquois were killed and 3 taken prisoner; another managed to escape by swimming away across the lake. Although this victory instilled new confidence in the colony's inhabitants, the hostilities did not cease until the signing of the Treaty of Montréal in 1701.

Year designated: 1925
Location: plaque erected on Senneville Road,
at the intersection of the Montée de l'Anse-à-l'Orme, Senneville.

THE ISLAND OF MONTRÉAL

110 Plaque commemorating the Battle of the Lake of Two Mountains.
Photo: Rémi Chénier, Parks Canada, Québec, 1991.

The Norseman

Canadian aviation had its hour of glory with the *Norseman*, a high-wing monoplane designed by Robert Noorduyn in 1935. Renowned for its sturdiness, reliability and excellent cargo capacity, this aircraft was very popular with bush pilots who flew in Canada's Far North. It was also adopted by many countries for commercial transport purposes. The *Norseman*'s builders, Noorduyn Aviation Ltd. and the Canadian Car & Foundry Co., designed several different versions of this airplane. Norseman IV and VI were used in large numbers by the Canadian and U.S. air forces during the Second World War.

Year designated: 1974
Location: Pierre Elliott Trudeau International Airport, 975 Roméo-Vachon Boulevard North, Dorval.

Sisters of Providence

This community was founded in 1843 by Émilie Tavernier, the widow of Jean-Baptiste Gamelin. The Sisters of Providence have been active in a range of areas for over 100 years, promoting the well-being of the sick and the underprivileged. Their ministry is thus multifaceted and involves running orphanages, hospitals, Amerindian schools, senior citizens' residences and so forth, and providing comfort and assistance to the sick, the poor, prisoners, the disabled and women who are victims of violence. The Sisters of Providence, whose institutions are renowned for the quality of their services, pursue with compassion the humanitarian work of their venerable founder.

Year designated: 1988
Location: plaque erected opposite the nuns' motherhouse, the Émilie-Gamelin Centre, 5655 de Salaberry Street, at the corner of De Meulles.

CARTIERVILLE

BOUL. GOUIN
RUE RANGER
Parc
de Mésy
RUE ÉMILE-NELLIGAN
RUE GRENET
RUE LACHAPELLE
BOUL. LAURENTIEN
RUE DE SALABERRY
RUE DE MEULES
RUE COUSINEAU

125
25

LAVAL

AUTOROUTE

25

LAURENTIDES

SAINT-MARTIN

19

440

GOUIN

112

117

HENRI-BOURASSA

15

40

DE LA CÔTE-VERTU

MONTRÉAL

AUTOROUTE CHOMEDEY

DE LA CÔTE-DES-NEIGES

111

520

20

DORVAL

AÉROPORT
INTERNATIONAL
PIERRE-ELLIOTT-TRUDEAU

RUE ROMÉO-VACHON
AV. MARSHALL
AV. MICHEL-JASMIN
AV. ORLY
AV. CARDINAL
AV. MARSHALL
520
20

Rivière des Prairies

PERRAS

LÉGER

HENRI-BOURASSA

ROUTE FÉLIX-LECLERC

NOTRE-DAME

113

RIVIÈRE-DES-PRAIRIES

PONT
CHARLES-DE-GAULLE

BOUL. GOUIN

128e AV.

Parc-nature de la
Pointe-aux-Prairies

132e
AV.

40

SAINT-MICHEL
SAUVÉ
PIE-IX
LACORDAIRE
AUTOROUTE MÉTROPOLITAINE
JEAN-TALON
VIAU
138
25
SAINT-DENIS
ROSEMONT
HOCHELAGA
SAINT-LAURENT
PAPINEAU
RUE SHERBROOKE
PONT JACQUES-CARTIER
132

PONT-TUNNEL
LOUIS-HIPPOLYTE-
LAFONTAINE

20

N

LONGUEUIL

GUY
720
10
WELLINGTON
NOTRE-DAME
15
20
PONT
VICTORIA

112

0   2   4 km ≈ 2.56 miles

13

The Battle
of Rivière-des-Prairies

113

In 1687 the Iroquois resumed their raids against settlements in New France, particularly in the Montréal region. It was against this background that the French and the Iroquois fought a battle that was later compared with the Long-Sault incident, near Carillon, for which Dollard Des Ormeaux is famous. In the summer of 1690 some 25 inhabitants of Rivière-des-Prairies, under the command of a former lieutenant of the French army, defeated around 100 Iroquois warriors who were about to attack Montréal. This event, which was long known as the *combat de la coulée Grou*, was first reconstructed by historian E.-Z. Massicotte. In 1914 he expressed the wish that a stele be erected to commemorate the battle. In June 1921 *Action française*, under the direction of Father Lionel Groulx, organized an historic pilgrimage to the site. Its national historic significance was recognized by the Historic Sites and Monuments Board of Canada in 1924.

Year designated: 1924
Location: plaque erected opposite 13470 Gouin Boulevard East, at the corner of 127e Avenue, Rivière-des-Prairies.

113 Plaque commemorating the Battle of Rivière-des-Prairies.
Photo: Rémi Chénier, Parks Canada, Québec, 1991.

111
112
113

THE ISLAND OF MONTRÉAL

ALPHABETICAL INDEX

Events
(and others)

Persons
(including groups)

Places
(including buildings)

THEMATIC INDEX

NOTES

Montréal, a City Steeped in History

_____
_____
_____
_____
_____
_____
_____
_____
_____
_____
_____
_____
_____
_____
_____
_____
_____
_____
_____
_____
_____
_____
_____
_____
_____
_____
_____
_____
_____
_____
_____
_____
_____
_____
_____

NOTES

NOTES

_____

_____

_____

_____

_____

_____

_____

_____

_____

_____

_____

_____

_____

_____

_____

_____

_____

_____

_____

_____

_____

_____

_____

_____

NOTES

NOTES

_____
_____
_____
_____
_____
_____
_____
_____

_____
_____
_____
_____
_____
_____
_____
_____
_____
_____
_____

_____
_____
_____
_____
_____
_____
_____
_____
_____
_____
_____

NOTES

NOTES